TRILBY JAMES

Trilby James read Drama at Bristol University before completing the three-year acting course at RADA. She graduated in 1990 and over the years has worked extensively as an actor in theatre and television. In 2000 she also began working as a freelance director and teacher at several leading drama schools including ALRA, Arts Educational Schools, Royal Central School of Speech and Drama, East 15, Mountview Academy of Theatre Arts, Manchester Metropolitan University and the Royal Academy of Dramatic Art where she is now an Associate Teacher. She continues to work across courses, directing third-year performances as well as teaching first and second-year students, MA students and running workshops for shorter programmes. She is a script reader and dramaturg for Kali Theatre Company and has directed several play-readings for their 'Talkback' seasons.

THE GOOD AUDITION GUIDES

AUDITION SONGS
edited by Paul Harvard

CONTEMPORARY DUOLOGUES
edited by Trilby James

CLASSICAL MONOLOGUES
edited by Marina Caldarone

CONTEMPORARY MONOLOGUES
edited by Trilby James

CONTEMPORARY MONOLOGUES FOR TEENAGERS
edited by Trilby James

SHAKESPEARE MONOLOGUES
edited by Luke Dixon

SHAKESPEARE MONOLOGUES FOR YOUNG PEOPLE
edited by Luke Dixon

The Good Audition Guides

CONTEMPORARY MONOLOGUES FOR TEENAGERS: FEMALE

edited and introduced by

TRILBY JAMES

NICK HERN BOOKS
London
www.nickhernbooks.co.uk

A NICK HERN BOOK

The Good Audition Guides:
Contemporary Monologues for Teenagers: Female
first published in Great Britain in 2019
by Nick Hern Books Limited
The Glasshouse, 49a Goldhawk Road, London W12 8QP

Introduction copyright © 2019 Trilby James
Copyright in this selection © 2019 Nick Hern Books Ltd

Designed and typeset by Nick Hern Books, London
Printed and bound by CPI Books (UK) Ltd

A CIP catalogue record for this book
is available from the British Library

ISBN 978 1 84842 608 5

Contents

6

Introduction

☞ WHAT THIS BOOK OFFERS

Whether you are taking theatre studies at school level,
auditioning for drama school or simply enjoying an after-
school drama group, a contemporary monologue that has been
specifically written for your own age group, and reflects the
concerns of young people, will be a great starting point. The
forty monologues in this volume are from plays that have been
written post-2000. The characters range in age from fourteen
to nineteen. There is a wide variety of character types and
styles of writing from which to choose. They are all drawn
from the extensive list of new plays published by Nick Hern
Books.

A Warning:

Some of the plays are specifically about the abuse of teenage
girls and may not be suitable for readers under sixteen. In the
theatre these parts would have been played by young adult
actors, so in this volume they come with the following trigger
warning: 'This play deals with adult themes. It has content
and language that some readers might find disturbing or
offensive.'

☞ CHOOSING YOUR MONOLOGUE

I have often likened finding the perfect monologue to finding
the perfect pair of jeans. It is rarely a case of 'one size fits all'.
You might have to try on several pairs, in different shops,
before you find the cut that works for you, but once you have,
you will feel confident in the knowledge that you are looking
and feeling your best. So it is with audition speeches. You
need to find pieces that suit you, that you cannot wait to get in
to and that will feel even better with wear.

If you are auditioning for a youth theatre:

- You will be judged on your potential and your willingness to be open, honest and free. Nobody is looking for a polished or over-rehearsed performance. It is best therefore to choose pieces that allow you to express yourself and for a panel to see something of who you really are.

- Choose something close to you in age and type. Something to which you can relate. Something that inspires you, from a play that speaks to you.

If you are auditioning for drama school:

- And have also been asked to prepare a classical speech, choose a contemporary monologue that will provide contrast. For example, you may have a Shakespearean monologue that is pensive or tragic, so opt for something comic. Similarly, if your classical speech is light in tone, choose a companion piece that shows off a more serious side.

If you are already at drama school:

- And you are looking to extend your range, you will want to choose a monologue that stretches you. Perhaps you are studying a particular accent or type of character quite different from yourself.

- Or you are looking for showcase material, think about how you wish to present yourself. Consider whether you are right for the part you have chosen and whether, if you had a chance to be in a production of the play, you could be easily cast in the role.

If you are auditioning for a specific role in a professional production (and have been asked to prepare an additional piece that is not from the play for which you are being seen):

- Choose something close to the part for which you are auditioning.

- Consider the language of the piece and whether you are after something heightened and obviously theatrical, or whether you require something more intimate and realistic.

If you are looking to extend your showreel:

- It may sound obvious, but think about what sort of speeches would be best suited to the varying demands of radio, film or television.

☞ PREPARING YOUR MONOLOGUE

- Learn your speeches well in advance of the actual audition. Should you forget your lines, the panel will be able to tell whether it is out of nervousness or insufficient preparation.

- Read the whole play. You may be asked questions about it or be required to improvise around it.

- Undertake all necessary research. Make a study of the historical, social and political world of the play. Be sure to understand the meaning of unfamiliar words and references.

- Accents: By and large it is best to avoid accents unless you are really good at them or want an opportunity to practise them. If a character's accent is not native to you, you may like to try playing it in your own accent. However, watch out for speeches that have been written with a strong dialect or idiom and where the essential rhythm of the piece needs to be maintained.

- Remain flexible in the way you perform/stage your monologue. Be prepared to be redirected in an audition.

- Talking to the audience: If your character is talking to the audience, make a decision about who the audience are to you. Are they your friend and your confidante? Are they more like an analyst with whom you feel safe to reveal your innermost thoughts? Are they a sort of sounding board? Are they judging you? Do you need to explain yourself or to convince them in some way? It is still advisable not to look at the actual panel in this case, but imagine an audience just above their heads and direct your speech there.

- Using props: There are no hard-and-fast rules about the use of stage properties at an audition. However, common sense suggests that, if you can easily carry an object in your pocket (e.g. a letter, a ring, a handkerchief, etc.), by all means bring this to an audition. If the object to which you refer is large, imagine it is there, or, if necessary, mime using it. Some might even argue that miming props is simpler, and in certain cases much more practical. In any event, you need not worry about being 'marked down' by your decision either to use real objects or to mime using them. What is important is that they do not become burdensome and get in the way of your acting.

- What to wear: Again there are no set rules about this, but I would suggest that to help you make a connection to your character you try to dress like them. If the character is formal or from another time in history, a dress or skirt as opposed to jeans and a T-shirt will make a huge difference. Similarly there is a very different feel when you wear hard shoes as opposed to trainers. When I was at drama school, our acting teacher used to refer to 'costume' as 'garments', and we would be encouraged to rehearse in appropriate clothing. In this way we thought of costume not as a thing that got added at the end, but as something that was as personal to us as our own everyday wardrobe.

- Try not to get stuck in a mode of delivery. It is useful to consider that, unless a character is making a political or after-dinner speech, chances are they have no idea they are going to speak for such a long time. They may make a statement, perhaps as a response to a specific question; then having made that statement they might need to qualify it. They might then be reminded of something else they wish to add and so on. In this way, a monologue can be regarded as a series of interrelated thoughts. Communicating a character's thought processes is fundamental to any acting technique. In the case of an audition, it takes the pressure off having to deliver a load of text. It allows you to stay fresh, to be in the moment and to make spontaneous choices. Before you start, all you need worry about is the trigger – the reason for saying what you do. Then have the courage to take it thought by thought and allow yourself to be surprised. In this way the monologue should feel slightly different every time.

- It is vital that you use your imagination to envisage all that the character sees and describes. If you are still seeing the page on which the speech is written, you know you are doing something wrong. Provide images for yourself so that in your mind's eye you quite literally lift the speech from the page.

- Timing/editing: Most speeches at audition should last no longer than two minutes. Some of the monologues in this volume are slightly longer, some shorter. Some I have cut, and some I have edited from dialogue with another character, and some have been augmented by joining two or more passages which appear separately in the original text. I have inserted this empty bracket symbol [...] to show where a cut has been made. Once you have read the whole play, you may have ideas of your own about what and what not to include.

☞ THE AUDITION

You will find there are many useful books on the market that make a complete study of this subject, from what to wear to how to enter and exit a room. These are some of the basics:

- Manage your nerves. Try to put the increased adrenaline you are experiencing to good use. Approach the audition with a positive sense of excitement, something to which you have been looking forward as opposed to something you have been dreading. Nervous energy, if correctly channelled, can help at an audition. Conversely you should avoid being under-energised. If you are someone who reacts lethargically to increased stress, you may need to do a good warm-up before you arrive.

- Take ownership of the situation. Before you begin, take a moment to imagine the space you are in as the location of the monologue. The best auditions are those in which the actor successfully transports the panel from 'Studio One' (or whatever the room you are auditioning in is called) to an urban street, a clearing in the woods, a grand room in a stately home, etc. Take time to think about where you will place the other character/s in the scene and, before you speak, allow yourself a moment to hear what has been said to you or to imagine what has just happened that prompts you to say the things you do. Do not rush the speech. Take your time. In the case of a drama-school audition, remember that you will be paying for this privilege!

- Empower yourself. There is no good reason why the panel should want you to fail. If you are auditioning for a youth group or a drama school, consider that the panel are willing you to do well, even if they are not necessarily giving that impression. If you have been asked to be seen for a specific role, it is because the director is serious about you for the job. It is possible that the panel are equally anxious about the impression they may give you. Remember, you only have control over your part of the audition process. There is no point speculating, worrying about whether they will want you in their group, grant you a place in their school or offer you the part. Just take care of your side of things, and be safe in the knowledge that, whatever happens, you tried your best.

☞ HOW TO USE THIS BOOK

For each of the monologues I have provided a bullet-point list of ten things you need to know about the character. These will include their age and where they come from, a bit about their background and what sort of personality they have. In some instances these facts are already contained within the monologue. Then I have suggested five things to help you perform the monologue. These will include objectives to play and ideas about how to connect to your character. They will also touch on the subjects already covered in this introduction such as using props, talking to the audience, accents and what to wear, etc. You will also need to read the whole play so that you can build a bigger picture. As you become increasingly familiar with your monologue, you will soon develop ideas of your own and may even find yourself in disagreement with my notes. Acting is a very personal thing, and no two actors, like any two people, will think exactly alike. I hope that this book will be a source of inspiration and ultimately get you thinking for yourself.

The Monologues

25% OFF
all the plays in this volume

All of the monologues in this collection are taken
from plays published by Nick Hern Books,
and can be ordered from:

www.nickhernbooks.co.uk

Use the following code at the checkout
and you will automatically receive 25% off any of the
titles featured in this volume:

NHBTEENMONOS

Happy reading!

A Hundred Words for Snow

Tatty Hennessy

TEN THINGS YOU NEED TO KNOW ABOUT RORY:

- Rory is fifteen years old.

- Her full name is Aurora, which she hates.

- She is an only child.

- She comes from a middle-class family.

- She lives in London.

- At this point in the play she is still a virgin.

- Her father has recently died following a car accident.

- He was a geography teacher at Rory's school.

- Rory was very close to her dad.

- Rory is clever, articulate and very funny.

FIVE THINGS TO HELP YOU PERFORM THE MONOLOGUE:

- Although she is grief-stricken, Rory can see a kind of black humour in what has happened. See if you can strike the balance between what is sad and very funny about the monologue.

- She is feisty and swears a lot. To what extent does this brashness help her to mask or to control her feelings of complete devastation? People react to death in very different ways, and grief can appear at very different times. Perhaps Rory is still in shock. Explore the possibility that the full impact of her father's death has not yet hit her. It was an accident, and unlike losing a parent who has been ill for a while, there has been no time for her to get used to the idea. Also, consider that her anger at the way the funeral was conducted, and at the mourners' reactions to it, is also part of her grieving process.

- Think about what you will use for the urn. As with all objects or props (see note on using props in the introduction), how you handle the urn will make a difference to the tone of the speech. Make a decision about how you will present the urn to the audience. It is, after all, a moment of great black comedy.

- Imagine what Rory's mum and dad look like. If you don't want to personalise her parents by using your own (which is understandable), make sure you have strong images in your mind so that you can really picture them. Perhaps there is even a male geography teacher at your own school or college that you could think of for Rory's dad. Imagine also the crematorium. If you have never been to one look up pictures online or better still visit one. It may sound a bit morbid, but they have a particular atmosphere, and it is important that you capture the uniqueness and peculiarity of the situation.

- As an only child, Rory has no sibling to share the pain, and her mother is so devastated that she cannot really help Rory at this point in the play. All this makes Rory very lonely. Read the whole play to see what happens when Rory attempts to take her dad's ashes to the North Pole.

NB This play offers several other monologues from which to choose.

Rory

❝ My name is Rory.

Yes, I know that's a boy's name.

Yes that is my real name.

Yes, really.

Oh, alright. Full name. If you really need to know; Aurora. Yes. Aurora.

Mortifying.

I swear the only people who like weird names are people with names like Bob or Sue or Tim. You like it? Try living with it.

It's weird to think Mum wanted me to be the kind of person who'd suit the name 'Aurora'. I wouldn't want to meet that person, would you? Sounds like a right bint.

I've totally forgiven her, as you can tell. Joking.

Nobody calls me Aurora. Call me Rory and we'll get on fine.

And this – (*The urn.*)

Is Dad.

Say hello, Dad.

Dad doesn't say anything.

He's shy.

RORY *gives us a small smile. She's testing us.*

Used to be a lot more talkative. Didn't you, Dad? Lost a bit of weight, too.

Balances the urn on her outstretched hand.

It's weird a whole person's in there.

This is Dad's story, really.

He died. Obviously. Car accident. Walking home from school. He's a teacher. At my school. I know. Mortifying. And a geography teacher. The worst. Sorry, Dad, but it's true. They didn't let me see the body before we got him cremated. I say 'we' but I didn't have anything to do with it, and actually if you ask me I think he'd've hated being inside a shitty urn for eternity but nobody did ask me did they so here he is. The funeral was fucking awful. The coffin like, slides behind these red curtains, and all I could think about was how many other people must've been burned in there and how unless they're really good at sweeping there's probably little bits of other people still in there with him and I wondered who they were and what their family thought about when the curtain shut. Mum did a reading but she was a total state, like, crying so much she couldn't even get the words out which was actually a blessing cos the poem she'd chosen was rubbish. He would've hated it. And all my dad's work friends which basically meant all my teachers coming to ours for sandwiches and relatives I never see saying empty things like 'oh well, wasn't it a lovely service' and I'm like actually my mum cried so much she couldn't string a sentence together and then they burned my dad in a fire so lovely isn't really the word for it, Aunt Carol.

I didn't say that. Obviously. I made the tea. People can't talk to you if you're busy making tea. And if they try you just say 'Sugar?' like that and they get distracted. I went to stand in the garden, just, breathe a bit and fucking Mum's out there. Crying. Again. Leaving me to talk to everyone by myself. Very responsible. **"**

Amongst the Reeds*

Chinonyerem Odimba

TEN THINGS YOU NEED TO KNOW ABOUT GILLIAN:

- Gillian is sixteen to seventeen years old.

- She is Vietnamese and speaks with a strong accent.

- She has recently given birth.

- Gillian was sent to the UK by her father, who trusted her uncle to provide an education for her. However, this did not happen, and she ended up not only sexually abused, but also a surrogate mother for a much older couple.

- When she ran away from her uncle she became increasingly attached to the baby and wanted to keep it for herself.

- She was befriended by a girl called Oni who is also an illegal immigrant. She and Oni have been living in a makeshift home in a disused office space. They have been in hiding.

- Once the baby was born, Gillian came out of hiding in the hope that the authorities would take care of her and her baby.

- Gillian is very trusting. She likes to see the good in people. This makes her vulnerable.

- She wants to be a good mother and a valuable member of society, but she will be rejected back in Vietnam, and in the UK she is the victim of an immigration system that is stacked against her.

- At only sixteen/seventeen, Gillian has been denied the normal life of a young girl growing up.

FIVE THINGS TO HELP YOU PERFORM THE MONOLOGUE:

- Gillian is determined to explain the truth about her situation. She believes that she will be looked after. See if you can find

* Published in the volume *House + Amongst the Reeds*

that trusting and hopeful quality at the very start of the monologue. How does that change as the monologue develops?

- Think about the official she is talking to. Make a decision about whether it is a man or a woman. What does he/she look like? What is the interview room like? How bright are those lights? Despite the fact that she is the real victim, she is being made to feel like the criminal.

- Think about all the other characters she refers to in the monologue. See if you can get a strong image in your mind of what they look like and about how they might make you feel.

- Gillian has only recently given birth. Think about not only the emotional but also the physical state she is in. Before you start the monologue imagine the sound of your baby's cry. Let it go right through you as if it is piercing your heart. It is often said that a mother can tell her child's cry from the sound of another's.

- She has come to the authorities for help, but they have taken her baby away. She is naturally distressed. Think about the overwhelming sense of shame she is feeling. Not only has she been coerced into having sex, she is now terrified of what her father will think of her.

NB This play offers a number of other monologues from which to choose.

Gillian

66 Where is my baby? Is she still here? I hear her cry.

I hear her cry and I am sure she crying for me.

Can I see her?

You know what I call her?

You have to call her by her name.

Stop her crying. Make her happy.

Her name is Victoria Beatrice.

Me and Oni choose it.

Gillian…

My name is Chi Anh Nguyen.

A strip light comes on –

GILLIAN *holds her hands up to shield her eyes from the light –*

Beat.

Please don't turn the light on.

I can see you without the light.

Please.

You don't understand the darkness is where I can see everything.

I don't want you to look at me this way…

No not boyfriend. Not boy. He doesn't have blue eyes. He is not young like me. A man.

A man that Uncle know. My uncle who my father trust to look after his daughter. He trust Uncle. His best friend for so long.

My father who put his girl on a plane to UK. My father trust Uncle to put me in study, look after me. He did for first few months but then when college ask for visa again in new term, he say he can't find passport. Then he say he have to get new passport. He doesn't care. Like he plan it. I say I want to go home but now this time my uncle start to say I have to do something for his friend. He say his friend good man. Him and his wife want baby but she is old, and so hard in UK to get baby. He say they pay a lot. Enough for new passport, and for me go back to study.

I have to stop school. The man come, and he come every day for many weeks. He come to the house all the time after work.

He try to be kind. He bring flowers and chocolate and sometimes he stay to talk after.

He always bring test for baby. Then one day test show two lines. He buy me takeaway food and give Uncle a car.

I grow big. I am very sick. Every day eat and sick. One day Uncle say man give him money to buy me clothes to look nice so we go shopping in centre with Uncle. I look in mirror and I can see it. Bump. It is getting bigger. I want it. I don't know. Maybe I don't want it…

I go to toilet and I see where you wash hands is window. I see the window and start climbing. I run so fast it feel like there is no ground. I don't see where until I stop.

Beat.

And before I am speaking to my father all the time on telephone. Uncle speak to him say visa coming soon. Now I don't tell my daddy. I can't tell him. My uncle tell him I leave my study and run away. He tell him that I am bad girl. Have many boyfriend.

How my father look at me now? Like prostitute?

Beat.

I want to be good for baby. I want to look after her now, Oni will help me.

Oni. Oni? My friend?

Me and my friend stay there together? She was there with me? She will tell you. She is a good person. Like my father…

Are you good person? Will you help me and baby? **99**

Amongst the Reeds*

Chinonyerem Odimba

TEN THINGS YOU NEED TO KNOW ABOUT ONI:

- Oni is seventeen.
- She is from Nigeria and speaks with a Nigerian accent.
- She was brought to the UK by her aunt who promised her a better life. However, when she arrived, she was treated like a slave and badly beaten.
- She ran away from her aunt and is applying for leave to remain in the UK, but she is not going to be successful.
- She is terrified of being deported back to Nigeria where her family will disown her.
- While she waits for legal status she is living in a makeshift home in a disused office block.
- She earns a bit of cash by doing black women's hairstyles.
- She has befriended a girl called Gillian, who is staying with her. Gillian is also living illegally in the UK. Gillian is Vietnamese and is heavily pregnant.
- Oni is kind, compassionate and caring. She wants to be a valuable member of society, but she will be rejected back in Nigeria, and in the UK she is the victim of an immigration system that is stacked against her.
- At only seventeen, Oni is both wise and old beyond her years.

FIVE THINGS TO HELP YOU PERFORM THE MONOLOGUE:

- Oni is scared, but she is also brave. See if you can find both these qualities when performing the monologue.
- Notice how determined she is. She is desperate for help, and refuses to give in.

* Published in the volume *House + Amongst the Reeds*

- She has experienced hardship and immense cruelty. Think about how lonely she must be with nowhere safe to go and no one safe to turn to.

- Think about the official she is talking to. Make a decision about whether it is a man or a woman. What does he/she look like? See if you can imagine what her auntie and cousin look like. Think about how her mother might look and what her life is like back home in Nigeria.

- A Scotch bonnet is a kind of chilli. It is so hot that it burns.

NB This play offers a number of other monologues from which to choose.

Oni

66 My name is Beatrice Oni Agbede.

You can see it dere. I am juss waiting for you to give me leave to remain. My solicitor told me to come here. She said that you have news for me about my application.

You believe me now don't you? You believe that I am not ar adult now don't you?

Did you speak to de headmistress at St Mary's School. Did she tell you what ar good student I used to be. Har favourite. She will have told you by now what year I was dere, maybe she even send de papers wiff my barth date?

I use my last one pound for bus juss to get here…

What is it?

Why are you looking at me like dat?

It is de same way dey look at me dat day aftar I go to police. But now you are looking at me like dis?

Beat.

What do you mean? Why do you want me to sign dere?

I am seventeen. I am seventeen…

Ask my school ageen. If I had my passport I would show you but she has taken everything from me.

Short beat.

What about my application? You can see dat can't you?

I ask you for help. You are meant to be helping me now. I tell dem, my solicitor, the officers everythin' about Auntie. I tell I run from har house. Scared for my life. I tell dem street no good but when someone hit your head wiff high-heel shoe, burn you wiff iron and…

And I ask them –

Do you know what Scotch bonnet feel like in your eye?

Who saw me? Who saw me enter dis country? Who saw me living in dat back room for months? Dis place dat is full of people you nevar see.

Please. I did not want to run away and do dis shame. She bring me here promising my modder she will look aftar me. She said dat to har. My kind auntie. Instead she find every excuse to beat me. Becuss har daughter's hair was not neat enough for school, becuss it is not clean enuff behind de toilet becuss becuss…

Please. Please you can't do dis!

If I go back I will shame my family. Do you not understand? If I go back dere is nothing for me to imagine any more. Everything will be over for me. I have wasted my only chance to do something good.

Please will you get someone. I know someone will have to believe me. I don't mind what odder tests you want to do. Please.

Please. I have never kissed ar boy. Never. I am ar virgin. You can do test. I am juss ar girl. I am ar good girl. **"**

August: Osage County

Tracy Letts

TEN THINGS YOU NEED TO KNOW ABOUT JEAN:

- Jean is fourteen.

- She is from the Midwest in America.

- She is an only child.

- She is a vegetarian.

- She is eccentric.

- She likes to shock, but it is important to note that the use of 'bad language' is common in the family.

- She is a film buff and loves old black-and-white movies.

- She is precocious. She likes talking about sex and pretending that she is older/more mature than she actually is. At one point in the play she even lies about her age and says that she is fifteen.

- She is lonely. Decide to what extent she smokes dope to hide her unhappy feelings.

- She craves attention. Again, make a decision about how this need for an audience makes up for the fact that her parents aren't always there for her.

FIVE THINGS TO HELP YOU PERFORM THE MONOLOGUE:

- The speech is very funny (enjoy the playfulness with which Jean communicates), but it is also sad, because her attempts to prove that she can cope with what is happening to her are just a front.

- Think about her voice and her physicality. Perhaps she has a particular way of speaking that makes her sound older than she is (or, that she *tries* to sound older), and similarly, she might move (or, *try* to move) more like a grown-up woman than a child.

- Jean is talking to Johnna the housekeeper. Johnna is twenty-six and is a Native American. She is the closest person in age to Jean. See if you can visualise what she looks like.

- Jean is lonely and is desperate for company. Notice how quickly she gets on to the subject of her parents and all that is troubling her.

- Make a decision about whether you will mime using a pipe, or use a real object (see note on using props in the introduction). Remember, that owing to our public smoking ban, you will have to *pretend* to light and smoke it!

Jean

❝ Hi. […] Am I bugging you? […] No, I thought maybe you'd like to smoke a bowl with me? […] Okay. I didn't know. Am I bugging you? […] Okay. Do you mind if I smoke a bowl? […] 'Cause there's no place I can go. Y'know, I'm staying right by Grandma's room, and if I go outside, they're gonna wonder— […] Mom and Dad don't mind. You won't get into trouble or anything. […] Okay. You sure?

From her pocket, JEAN takes a small glass pipe and a clear cigarette wrapper holding a bud of marijuana. She fixes the pipe.

I say they don't mind. If they knew I stuck this bud under the cap of Dad's deodorant before our flight and then sat there sweating like in that movie Maria Full of Grace. Did you see that? […] I just mean they don't mind that I smoke pot. Dad doesn't. Mom kind of does. She thinks it's bad for me. I think the real reason it bugs her is 'cause Dad smokes pot, too, and she wishes he didn't. Dad's much cooler than Mom, really. Well, that's not true. He's just cooler in that way, I guess.

JEAN smokes. She offers the smoldering pipe to Johnna.

(*Holding her breath.*) You sure? […] No, he's really not cooler. (*Exhales smoke.*) He and Mom are separated right now. […] He's fucking one of his students which is pretty uncool, if you ask me. Some people would think that's cool, like those dicks who teach with him in the Humanities Department because

they're all fucking their students or wish they were fucking
their students. 'Lo-liii-ta.' I mean, I don't care and all, he can
fuck whoever he wants and he's a teacher and that's who
teachers meet, students. He was just a turd the way he went
about it and didn't give Mom a chance to respond or anything.
What sucks now is that Mom's watching me like a hawk, like,
she's afraid I'll have some post-divorce freak-out and become
some heroin addict or shoot everybody at school. Or God
forbid, lose my virginity. I don't know what it is about Dad
splitting that put Mom on hymen patrol. Do you have a
boyfriend? […] Me neither. I did go with this boy Josh for like
almost a year but he was retarded. Are your parents still
together? […] Oh. I'm sorry. […] Oh, fuck, no, I'm really
sorry, I feel fucking terrible now. […] Oh God. Okay. Were
you close with them? […] Okay, another stupid question
there, Jean, real good. Wow. Like: 'Are you close to your
parents?' […] Yeah, right? So that's what I meant. Thanks. **"**

*NB You will have to imagine Johnna's responses to Jean's two
questions, 'Are your parents still together?' and 'Were you close to
them?', in order for the speech to flow. Where there are now brackets
[…] to denote a cut, the unedited text reads as follows:*

JEAN. Are your parents still together?

JOHNNA. They passed away.

JEAN. Oh. I'm sorry.

JOHNNA. That's okay. Thank you.

JEAN. Oh, fuck, no, I'm really sorry, I feel fucking terrible now.

JOHNNA. It's okay.

JEAN. Oh God. Okay. Were you close with them?

JOHNNA. Yeah.

JEAN. Okay, another stupid question there, Jean, real good. Wow.
Like: 'Are you close to your parents?'

JOHNNA. Not everybody is.

JEAN. Yeah, right? So that's what I meant. Thanks.

Bird

Laura Lomas

This play deals with adult themes. It has content and language that some readers might find disturbing or offensive.

TEN THINGS YOU NEED TO KNOW ABOUT LEAH:

- Leah is fourteen.
- In the play she is speaking from a dilapidated flat in Hartington Street, Derby (an area that is known for its poverty and social deprivation). Therefore the monologue would work well in any accent that reflected a similar environment.
- The play deals with the sexual abuse of vulnerable young girls, and Leah is extremely vulnerable.
- Leah is very trusting, and it is in her nature to see the best in people.
- Leah is in love with an older man called Sammy. Sammy lies to her. He says he wants to move to London with her so that they can live together, but later on in the play she will admit to us that he already has a partner and a child. Although she doesn't want to acknowledge it, he's only interested in her for sex and for pimping her out to other men. 'Sammy' is not even his real name.
- Sammy keeps her down by giving her weed, alcohol and sleeping pills, and she is bruised from where he physically and sexually mistreats her.
- Leah's mother is dead. They were very close. Leah misses her; without her mother to support and guide her, Leah is lost.
- She lives with her stepdad and younger sister, Charlie. Since the death of her mother, life at home hasn't been the same. Sammy has promised to take Charlie with them to London, but this is another lie.
- She has a best friend called Carla, who talks non-stop. However, Carla doesn't approve of her relationship with Sammy, and the girls fall out.

- Even though she is still a child, Leah is desperate to appear like an adult. She loves it when Sammy refers to her as a 'woman'. It makes her feel good about herself, and she can forget about her pain. Like a lot of emotionally vulnerable people, Leah likes to appear tough. This outer shell is a mask or protection from the hurt she feels inside.

FIVE THINGS TO HELP YOU PERFORM THE MONOLOGUE:

- The whole play is a monologue and Leah is very aware of her audience. This extract comes from the very beginning of the play. She talks directly and openly to us. Don't be afraid to engage with your audience. Think about how lonely Leah is and why speaking to us is so important to her. She really needs us on her side.

- Leah has become completely dependent on Sammy. Even though a huge part of her knows he is lying, she doesn't want to believe it. She is in denial. Perhaps you know that feeling of pretending to yourself that everything is okay, even when, deep down, you know it isn't. Also, without overplaying it, think about how she is unable to think clearly because of all the alcohol and pills she takes.

- She likes to appear tough, but it is pretty obvious that she isn't. See if you can capture that 'hard on the outside/soft on the inside' quality.

- Have a very strong image in your head about what Sammy looks like. How does he dress? Perhaps she has convinced herself that he is better looking than he actually is. Although you have never met Sammy's dad, imagine what *he* might look like. Sinfin is a suburb of Derby. If you decide to change where Leah comes from, you will need to substitute another place name for authenticity.

- Think about where you are and the state of the flat. What does it look like? How does it smell? How does it make you feel to be here on your own?

NB This play offers a number of other monologues from which to choose.

Leah

❝ I know what you're thinking.

Pause.

Don't look at me like that, course I know. I always know, I ain't stupid.

Beat.

You don't think I know? You don't think I see it? Way you give me them eyes…

Thinking 'why don't she just leave? Door's over there'. Thinking 'look at her, all dressed up, waiting for her boyfriend to come, as if he's gonna come, four in the morning as if he's even coming for her now', thinking I'm stupid, thinking I'm kiddin' myself, thinking I got nothing but air in my head, is that it? Is that what you're thinking?

Beat. LEAH *looks a little bruised.*

Yeah, well… you people don't know shit.

She walks over to her phone and picks it up.

Sammy ain't text me yet.

Beat.

It's okay, I ain't bothered. I only been here like one hour, it ain't a big deal.

She looks at her phone again. Looks back at us.

I was just walking round town for a bit…

And right… I ain't gonna lie, at first… at first I was upset… okay, at first I was thinking bad thoughts, an', an', an' –

At first I was thinking maybe I done something wrong, cus I couldn't remember. I couldn't remember, everything was so… in my head was so…

Her whole body tenses. Beat.

That's why I called him. To talk to him, hear his voice. Calm me… an' at first when he don't pick up, I was thinking shit –

what if something happen to him and the idea of it make me panic so bad I could feel my heart beating right in my throat.

That's why I come here. To get my head straight. Sort my thoughts out, stop 'em banging round my head like a fuckin' machine gun going off.

She looks around the room, looks back at us.

I sat on the bed and tried him again, and this time… The phone just go dead.

I know what you're thinking, that he switch it off on me? An' I was thinking it too, cus all of a sudden I start panicking and I'm sat there with my head in my hands, breathing, trying to keep calm, counting to like thirty.

That's when I remember.

'Bout his situation. How he's always like 'Leah, don't be callin' me late.'

Sammy live with his dad in one of them new houses down Sinfin. He don't like it, he wants to get away, he says he's tired of looking after him, he want his own life too, don't he?

Sammy say his dad is weird, say he don't like the phone, don't like people callin' him. Tell me once when him and his dad was in Asda Sammy's phone kept goin' an' his dad start stressin' so bad, he thought he was gonna have a heart attack, right there in the bread aisle, near the baguettes, he swear down.

Beat. She looks down at her phone.

I text him,

Said 'Hey Babe, I don't mean to keep calling you, but just to let you know… I'm here. I'm at the flat.

I'm waiting for you,
I hope you come get me soon.'

She pauses, summing up whether to tell us.

Then I put

'I'm sorry.'

'I love you'

and a kiss.

Beat. She shifts.

He ain't replied to me yet but it's only cus he's busy. **99**

Blue Stockings

Jessica Swale

TEN THINGS YOU NEED TO KNOW ABOUT TESS:

- The year is 1896.

- Tess is about eighteen.

- She comes from a middle-class family.

- Tess is in her first term studying science at Girton College, Cambridge. Girton was the first college in Britain to admit female students, and 1896 saw the first intake.

- Tess and her fellow female students experience immense opposition, particularly from the male students at Cambridge, who verbally abuse and bully them.

- Tess is known as a 'bluestocking'. It was a negative term to describe a woman who was educated and therefore unnatural and unmarriageable.

- Tess is described as 'a curious girl'. She very quickly got into trouble for expressing views that her male lecturers considered outrageous.

- Unlike some of the other girls, Tess is conflicted between her studies and remaining fit for marriage, and she is fully aware of the risks an education brings. A part of her longs for love and romance, and another part knows that being a wife and mother would not be enough for her.

- One day in the library she met Ralph Mayhew, a student at Trinity College. They exchanged notes and secretly agreed to meet in the orchard at night. Tess fell in love with Ralph and considered abandoning her studies. However, although Ralph professed to love her back, he had no intention of marrying her and is now engaged to someone else.

- Tess has a friend from home called Will. Will is a student at King's College. While Will is supportive of Tess's education, it is hard for him to be seen to do so when he is in the company of other male students.

FIVE THINGS TO HELP YOU PERFORM THE MONOLOGUE:

- Consider the historical context. This is a time that saw the emergence of women as free-thinking individuals, in search of lives other than those of being a wife and mother. Make time to research the struggles of these women and how Girton College came to exist in the first place, and to understand the phenomenal bravery of those who fought for this right.

- Tess has only just heard from her friend Will that Ralph is engaged to someone else. The monologue that follows is therefore very raw. Tess is reacting to what must feel like a stab in the heart. She wasn't even aware that she and Ralph had finished. She is humiliated and betrayed, but above all she feels like a failure. Perhaps you can relate to this kind of heartache or have observed it in someone you know.

- Tess is talking to her friend and fellow student, Celia. Imagine Celia as someone *you* are close to. You could even try practising the piece out loud with that person.

- Tess's immediate reaction is to run away. The reason is two-fold. Firstly the thought of being anywhere near Ralph must fill her with dread, and secondly the idea of carrying on studying and being a 'bluestocking' will mark her for life. (In a short while, Celia will convince her otherwise, but for now she wants to quit.)

- Tess has not been averse to risk. How might this compare to your own desire to be in plays or even to be a professional actor one day? Have you felt resistance from anyone or do you doubt whether you will succeed? If you recognise these sensations they will be very useful in allowing you to connect to Tess's restlessness, her dream of an education and her fear of disappointment. Also what happens when love gets in the way? Have you ever not been able to think clearly or concentrate because you are too distracted?

Tess

❝ There was a girl at home. Lived at the parsonage. Annabel. She'd spend a whole afternoon sewing a ribbon onto a bonnet, and she'd be content. Why wasn't that enough for me, Celia? You know, I'd climb the roof of Will's classroom just to listen. Once I lost my footing and they found me hanging by my underskirt, but I wouldn't let go of my notebook. I should have fallen and cracked my skull right then and there, I'd have been better off.

But no. I was stubborn. Forfeit any hope of reputation, of a good match, wreck Mother's nerves with worry, all for this, to be here. And then I meet a boy. A poet. A poet! In a library. And I fall for him like a rock. And suddenly I can't think because my mind is full of him. I read Keats and hear his voice. I look at Vermeer and there he is, in oils. And I love him with every thought and bone and sinew. And then he buys a ring. But it's not for me. And now. What am I now? He's caved out my heart, Celia. What do I do? I've got nothing left. **❞**

Bodies

Vivienne Franzmann

TEN THINGS YOU NEED TO KNOW ABOUT THE DAUGHTER:

- The Daughter is sixteen.

- She is called 'Daughter' in the script because when she appears on stage it is as a voice or presence from the future.

- In terms of the timeline of the play, she is yet to be born and therefore hasn't been named.

- She is the daughter of Clem and Josh. Josh is her biological father, but the egg comes from a donor in Russia, which, once fertilised, has been placed in the womb of a surrogate in India. (It's a bit complicated and you will need to read the whole play to understand more.)

- The Daughter is angry. At sixteen she is transitioning from girl to woman and is starting to question her identity.

- She argues a lot with Clem and is often unkind to her 'mother'.

- She swears a lot and is dismissive of her teachers.

- She is a fussy eater and worries about things like trans fats.

- Just before her birth, the law in India was changed, banning foreign couples from employing surrogates. However, she was 'conceived' before the new legislation, and was allowed to go to the UK.

- The surrogate in India sacrificed the wellbeing of her own daughter in order to provide for Clem and Josh. When she heard about the ban she tried to abort the baby before she was born. In many ways, the Daughter is symbolic of how the developed world exploits poor countries to serve their own selfish ends.

- The Daughter is talking to her mother, Clem. The Daughter is a kind of projection into the future. She appears as a warning of what might happen. Be aware of this 'out of time' quality while appearing as if you are living now.

- She says she wants to help Clem by protecting her from the difficult questions that one day she will have to answer. However, her tone is also accusatory. See if you can balance her desire to make Clem understand, with her own personal rage at not knowing who she is.

- The final line, 'Then you never would have – Bought me', should come as a real sting in the tail. The fact that money had to change hands, that her birth was part of a business transaction, seems to be the thing she detests the most. It is also reflective of Clem's guilt at how her surrogate had to sacrifice the wellbeing of her own children.

- See if you can picture what Clem looks like. You might like to imagine someone who looks very different from you. Perhaps there is a teacher at school or a friend of your mother's, or the mother of a friend of yours. Really imagine that you are talking to this person.

- Unless you yourself have been adopted or conceived with the aid of a donor, it may be difficult to understand fully the need for the Daughter to recognise where she has come from. Take time to consider the implications of such a situation. Most of us take our identity for granted.

Daughter

❝ What part of me belongs to you?

—

Which bits of me are yours? I can tell you exactly what's Daddy's. The maths, the jokes, the spatial awareness and the art stuff.

—

When are you going to tell me? Right from the start so it's not a shock? Or when you think I'm old enough to understand? Or maybe you'll let me find out myself by accident when I need my birth certificate. You know, bury the landmine and wait for me to stumble on it.

—

You must have thought about how it will affect me.

—

You must have.

—

I'm trying to help you. Because I'll want to know. I'll want to know why I don't look you. And why I don't act like you. Or think like you or feel like you. Why I feel a million miles away from you when you're supposed to be my mother. I'll look at you and I won't know who I am.

—

Who am I?

—

Look at me.

—

Are you more like your mum or your dad?

—

I said are you – [...] I think you're a daddy's girl like me. [...] But maybe not, because – [...] If you were a daddy's girl – [...] Then you never would have – [...] Bought me. 〝

Broken Biscuits

Tom Wells

TEN THINGS YOU NEED TO KNOW ABOUT MEGAN:

- Megan is sixteen years old.

- She comes from Withernsea, which is a small town near Hull, on the east Yorkshire coast.

- She lives with her mum, dad and older brother.

- It is the summer holidays, and she has just finished her GCSEs.

- She is not particularly good at school, but is hoping to scrape a pass so that she can go to sixth-form college.

- Megan describes herself as 'all fat, and gobby'. This is true, but although she sometimes speaks before she thinks, she doesn't mean anybody any harm.

- She is unhappy with the way she looks because she gets picked on and called names, and she would love just to be considered normal.

- There is the suggestion in the play that she is no longer a virgin. However, we get the impression that whoever it was she slept with is no longer interested in her and even ignores her.

- Her best friends are Ben and Holly. Ben is gay and Holly is a geek. All three of them struggle to fit in.

- Her dream is to start a band so that they will become cool, popular and no one will think they are losers.

FIVE THINGS TO HELP YOU PERFORM THE MONOLOGUE:

- You will need to think of ways to create the drum kit if you don't have access to one. Why not try putting a few chairs of varying sizes together. If you can get some drum sticks that would help to create the impression. Follow the stage directions and place a large sheet over it so that you can play the 'reveal'.

- Think about her accent and the way she speaks. If you don't come from Yorkshire, try playing it in your own accent, but remember that she is loud, and excitable.

- Her main objective is to free herself (and Ben and Holly) from being 'losers'.

- Popularity is a big deal, especially at sixth-form college, and she genuinely believes that they can become cool, and therefore happy, by being in a band.

- The speech is very funny. It requires energy. Without rushing it, see if you can find the necessary rhythm and pace. Consider the way some sentences are really long and others are really short. She is super-excited and therefore erratic or even hyper.

- Have a strong sense of what Ben and Holly look like. Although Megan is in her own world and not very good at listening, it will help you to know where to focus your attention. You might like to imagine their reactions.

Megan

❝ Get ready for your whole lives to completely change for ever.

MEGAN *pulls the sheet off to reveal a drum kit.*

TA-DAH! […] I know.

She chucks the old sheet to one side. […]

I know. […] I can't actually play them yet. The drums. […] I literally just saw them in the window, the hospice shop, saw them sitting there in the window, twenty quid, the lot, which I actually hung on a couple of days, talked them down to fifteen cos they're quite bulky, the woman in the shop wanted rid. Said people kept just going in, playing them dead loud, it was doing her head in. […] Anyway, I was like: fifteen quid, I'm having them. Yoink. Goodbye being a shitty overweight nobody. Hello rhythm. […] Got them home, which actually took quite a lot of doing, I had to nick a trolley from Aldi, but I thought: it'll be worth it. It'll all be worth it when I get them set up, start bashing out some sweet sweet beats like a fucking, I dunno. Drummer. So I did. Got them back here, just in my room to begin with but then my mum was like: genius idea, Megan, why don't you try putting them in the shed? That way, we won't be disturbing you so much, probably won't even be able to hear you, hardly. And I was like: good call, Wendy. Good call. […] I'm calling her Wendy for a bit, cos I'm mature and that. She's not enjoying it. But I'm just like: Wendy... Anyway, got them in here, cleared like a space and, yeah. That's it. So... […] We're fucking, doing it! Aren't we though? A band! We're doing a band! Fist-bump. Fist-bump. 〞

Brute*

Izzy Tennyson

TEN THINGS YOU NEED TO KNOW ABOUT POPPY:

- Poppy is fourteen years old.

- She comes from a middle-class background.

- She lives with her mum, dad and older sister. The family has recently moved back to England from Spain.

- When Poppy was in Spain she went to an expensive independent school. Now that she is back in England she goes to an all-girls state school in a provincial town. It has come as a shock to Poppy to have to start over in a new school where the girls already know each other. Friendship groups are tight, often brutal, and it is hard for Poppy to fit in.

- Back in Spain she preferred the company of boys and was good at football.

- Her father used to earn a lot of money. Now that he doesn't he spends most of his time sitting in the attic. Poppy says she hardly knows him.

- Her mother is also depressed. Poppy thinks it is because they have a lot less money than they used to.

- Poppy is dyslexic. She is highly articulate but doesn't do well at school. She describes herself as 'thick as shit', but strictly speaking this isn't true.

- When she was in Spain, Poppy was sexually assaulted by an old man who used to look after their dog. Poppy recognises that this event, along with the family upheaval, has led to her feeling isolated, angry and depressed.

- Poppy is highly observant, and self-reflective. She is emotionally intelligent, and although she doesn't always behave her best, she knows when she has overstepped the mark.

* Published in the volume *Grotty & Brute* by Izzy Tennyson

- The whole play is one long monologue so there may be other sections that you would like to perform. This speech comes at the very start of the play and is Poppy's way of introducing herself to us. (See note on talking to the audience in the introduction.) In some ways it is a bit like a stand-up routine. Poppy is always honest, very funny and unafraid to show us her shortcomings and vulnerability. See if you can find this self-deprecating quality which makes the play so funny, touching and sad.

- Perhaps you have had a similar experience of starting at a school later than everyone else. With friendship groups already formed, it can be a very lonely and frightening experience. The title of the play, *Brute*, gives an indication of how cruel girls can be. Poppy also includes herself in that sort of unkind behaviour. You will need to connect to Poppy's feelings of isolation and also gratitude that there are some girls who have welcomed her.

- Take time to consider what life was like in Spain. It was a time when her dad was earning a lot of money. They had a big house, perhaps with a swimming pool – and the days would have been sunny and very hot in the summer. In many ways it would have been idyllic, but when you read on you will discover that Poppy was sexually molested in Spain. You can't actually play all of that, but in order to create some inner life for yourself you will need to understand how confused she is.

- Think about the significance of the dogs and how the move back to England is associated with their potential death. Perhaps the move from Spain to England feels like a mini death to Poppy as well.

- The monologue takes in a number of different people and locations and even time frames. Be clear about what has happened to you when and where, and use your imagination to picture all that she describes.

NB This play offers a number of other monologues from which to choose.

Poppy

❝ I keep forgetting I have dogs. You know? It's weird, because I don't really see the point of having them. Not any more. My mum sat down and explained to me, that there is a possibility, because they're old, that they might die on the plane. In the boxes. I imagine them arriving to the house and we open the box that they were packaged in and there are just dead dogs in there. But I find it funny, because it would be so tragic. You know? I don't know if it would just be easier if we just sort of just left them there. It was an option, you know, to leave them. Planes cause serious stress to animals. But my mum wouldn't have that, because she really loves those dogs. She said it was selfish really, on her part. But you want them too don't you? And I said yeah I do, I do want them. (*Pause.*) The thing is we might have killed them, you know.

POPPY *starts getting dressed for school.*

You know I don't know one boy in England. I don't know one boy in the whole of England. Not one. I used to be only with boys in Spain, at Newtons, my school. My mum loved that. Poppy and her boys. She used to give us lifts to football. I loved football, I was the only girl who played, and I used to be picked last, for the teams that is, but then, when I got better, I was actually really, really good, I got picked third. And that's because you have to pick your strikers first, then defence. Mum said maybe Poppy, maybe that's why you're not having a good time at the moment, because you've always gotten on better with boys. Always…

Pause.

I've got a group now, who were in my form group, they were there all along. I had to sit with Natalie Danes and Becca Carr for a bit. They sat outside the science labs by the massive bins. But I just stopped meeting them, and they haven't said anything. No I'm with Danielle, well Dani, who actually is the one who showed me around. On the first day.

So it's fine. Dani's proper nice though, she's a bit like the gentle giant. She's like massive, and everything is a bit muddled, she's like a jigsaw puzzle that hasn't been put together properly. Everything is a bit out of proportion you know, like she's got very broad shoulders and her boobs look like they're too high up just under her collarbone, and really long legs so she towers over me. And her eyebrows are huge, like caterpillars, but her eyes are tiny and her mouth is really long. I wonder if it's all going to come together at some point, because it's not right at the moment. She's so strong, like once she pushed me, like joking and I proper flew across the playground.

She likes David Beckham, and that's how we got talking about it. I once got into a detention because I touched David Beckham's car. He came to have a look at the school in Spain, to take his kids there, when he was playing in Real Madrid, and I was waiting by the road outside to get picked up and his car was parked there and my headmaster came out because I was standing next to it, and he thought I was waiting for Beckham, when I was just waiting for my mum. And I got a detention. I was leaning against the car, you see. Actually this didn't happen to me it happened to my older sister but I tell it like it happened to me anyway. People like the story. She tells it better than me because she was actually there. So I sit with them now. Dani's lot, well it's more like Chloe's lot. I'm with Chloe's lot now. **99**

Crushed Shells and Mud

Ben Musgrave

TEN THINGS YOU NEED TO KNOW ABOUT LYDIA:

- Lydia is seventeen.

- She has been infected by a deadly disease that is ripping its way through the United Kingdom.

- Her parents have abandoned her, and she is being protected by a secret network of carers who help those with the virus.

- In order to keep her safe, they have moved her from place to place so as not to be discovered. She is now in a seaside village on the east coast of England in a safe house.

- At the start of the play she met Derek (to whom she speaks in the monologue). He is described as being 'not in her league'. From this we assume that she is attractive and sophisticated in a way that 'townies' or privileged people are.

- The disease has left her with a black mark on her upper body. It is the telltale sign that she has been infected.

- She has no idea whether she will live or die, and regularly has to inject herself with medicine.

- This uncertainty has made her less careful. She smokes, drinks and does drugs because she has nothing to lose.

- Because of her condition and fears for the future she is prone to mood swings. There are times when she feels positive and others when she feels bleak. Read the whole play to understand more.

- Because she has on the surface a 'fit' body, and has trained to be a dancer, it is doubly difficult for her to come to terms with what has happened.

FIVE THINGS TO HELP YOU PERFORM THE MONOLOGUE:

- This is the first time in the play that we hear about what happened to Lydia. It comes quite late on in the story. Think, therefore, about the enormity of this 'confession'. Although vulnerable, she has come to trust Derek and feels safe with him.

- Imagine what Derek looks like. Perhaps you have experienced a similar relationship that wasn't initially passionate on your part, but has got stronger over time.

- It is unlikely that you will have experienced a similar trauma and/or been abandoned in this way. As the play is part fantasy, you will need to use your imagination to understand the gravity of the situation. It may help to remember when you were last ill and times it by a thousand!

- Take time to think about Robbie. What did he look like? Make a decision about why she pauses before saying, 'he was my… particular friend'.

- Lydia is guilty. On some level she blames herself for acquiring the disease and for all that followed. See if you can capture this feeling of shame coupled with an intense rage and loneliness, then, read the whole play to discover its positive ending. When you are working on sad or tragic monologues it is important not to get down yourself. When you know what happens in the end, you will feel less sad about the world of the play.

Lydia

❝ I read your story. […]

The one about the trawlerman.
You remember you gave it to me?

When we first met? […]

I loved it. […]

I thought it was wonderful.

I felt like you'd really understood his feelings.

Like you'd got under his skin.

It was gorgeous. [...]

Pause.

Before Sussex.

I was at a dance academy in London.
We felt very free there, all of us.
Every day we had to have courage.
To be and feel how we wanted to be.
To touch others
To understand the bodies of others.
It wasn't wrong, it was lovely.
I felt that I was discovering things every day.

[...]

There was a boy called Robbie, and he was my... particular friend.
I was fifteen and he was seventeen, and I had sex with him.
Before the panic.
Before it emerged.
We weren't careful enough.
I was on the pill.

I didn't know that he'd slept with other girls before me!
We were just young!
Then he got very ill and died.
And other people at the academy.

And then I got very ill.
And my parents
Couldn't handle it.

And started to reject me.
And wouldn't come near me.
And wouldn't hug me.
And that's when it was born inside me.

Pause. She struggles with it.

And one day they were gone.
On a business trip, they said.
And they put me in a hospital.
And they didn't come.
And when the hospital made enquiries
It turned out my mother and father had left the country.

Pause.

Will you go swimming again, Derek? 〞

Echoes*

Henry Naylor

TEN THINGS YOU NEED TO KNOW ABOUT SAMIRA:

- Samira is seventeen.

- She is a British Muslim.

- She comes from Ipswich in Suffolk.

- She hates where she lives and longs to escape.

- She is intelligent, savvy and has a strong sense of humour.

- She is sensitive to the suffering of other Muslims, and genuinely wants to help them and make a difference to the world.

- She is courageous and dutiful.

- Her family are religious, but they are not fundamental in their beliefs.

- Samira on the other hand is easily influenced and would be prepared to make sacrifices for her beliefs.

- You will need to read the whole play to see what happens to her when she makes the dangerous journey to Iraq.

FIVE THINGS TO HELP YOU PERFORM THE MONOLOGUE:

- The speech is part of a much longer monologue. This section comes at the very start of the play and sets up the story of how Samira became radicalised. Read the whole play – there may be other parts that you would like to perform. If you like this first section, think about why she needs to tell us what happened to her in the first place (and see note on talking to the audience in the introduction). Once you have read the whole play you will see that her story serves as a stark warning to other young Muslim women who may be attracted

* Published in the volume *Arabian Nightmares* by Henry Naylor

to becoming 'Jihadi brides'. Use this need to warn us as the impetus or objective for starting the monologue.

- Samira has a very direct way of talking and communicating. From the very first line she is up-front, feisty and challenging. Look at the way she calls us 'kuffar' – 'non-believers' or 'infidel'. See if you can capture her tone.

- The monologue is both funny and serious. The way she uses humour by joking about Ipswich and popular magazine culture helps us to understand what might attract an intelligent woman to something that seems more worthy and meaningful than worrying about what she looks like in a bikini. The humour also acts as a kind of line that draws us, the audience, in – providing a contrast to what is actually a very dark and serious story.

- Think about her friend Beegum. What does she look like? How does she speak? Perhaps you too have a friend who is really into politics or global issues. Do they ever make you feel shallow or ignorant? It is interesting to note that Samira can trace back the exact moment of her 'awakening' to selling her friend the mouse mat. What did that mouse mat look like? It may seem like a silly question, but it is these precise details and associations that will bring depth to your playing.

- Take time to visualise all that she mentions or describes. There are many well-known people that she talks about. Make sure you know who they are and what they look like. What might a 'Syrian basement' be like? You probably know what WHSmith is like. If you don't know Ipswich look up images on the internet. It was heavily bombed during the Second World War. Do you remember the dress that in some lights looked blue/black and in others white/gold? Research it if not – the debate became a viral sensation. You will also need to familiarise yourself with the ongoing wars and interventions in the Middle East.

NB This play offers a number of other monologues from which to choose.

Samira

❝ I know what you're thinking:
'Why would a Grade-A student suddenly upsticks to become
a housewife in a Syrian basement?'
Ha. You kuffar don't understand Faith, do you?
This is my choice: Paradise... or Ipswich.
The first: the shadow of God's kingdom on earth.
The second: a land of chip papers and dogshit.
You choose.

Wasn't always religious. Used to be shy, quiet.
A good student.
Until the day I sold Beegum a mousemat in WHSmith's...

My Saturday job is manning the till, stacking the shelves, in
the News and Magazines section.
...Embarrassing to have to serve my devout schoolfriend.
'Man, how can you sell this shit?' She waves her hand over the
newsracks.
'What's wrong with it?'
'Kuffar press is full of lies. Only times Muslims get
mentioned is when they're beheading people. Never anything
about the Syrian refugees, or drone strikes killing babies.'
She may have a point;
the front pages are often about Kim Kardashian's bottom.
'So how come *you* know about refugees, and baby-seeking
missiles?'
'Internet.'
'The internet!?! There's people on the internet says that dress
is blue/black rather than white/gold.'
'It is.'
'How can you say that?? It's white/gold.'
'Blue/black.'
...'White/Gold.'

Lunchtime, I look up 'Syrian refugees' on my smartphone.
There are three-point-eight million of them.

I pretend to tidy the shelves. Flick through a tabloid. Mostly
the Election and Nigel Farage.

…The refugees only appear on page eleven. After an advert asking whether I'm Beach Body Ready.

In another, there are no refugees.

Instead, there's a whole page of Katie Hopkins. Flapping her mouth like a bag lady.

As the customers come and lay their papers on the counter, I want to grab them and shout: 'Are we not human to you?'

But what I actually say is: '…do you want the vouchers?' 🙶

Echoes*

Henry Naylor

TEN THINGS YOU NEED TO KNOW ABOUT TILLIE:

- Tillie is seventeen.

- She comes from an upper-middle-class background.

- It is the nineteenth century, and Tillie is a Victorian pioneer woman.

- She is described as 'strong and smart'.

- Tillie comes from Ipswich in Suffolk.

- She lives with her parents and has an older brother who has spent five years in India.

- In many ways Tillie is ahead of her time. She is educated and curious, and longs to leave the confines of her family and home.

- Tillie has a strong sense of right and wrong and hates any social injustice.

- She has high principles and believes in the might and rule of the British Empire, until she travels abroad and sees the brutality of the British at first hand.

- Tillie is immensely brave. Unlike the other women in her social circle, when her husband becomes violent, she refuses to obey his commands and rebels against his brutish behaviour.

FIVE THINGS TO HELP YOU PERFORM THE MONOLOGUE:

- Her accent and way of speaking is a crucial component. She is 'posh' and the language is heightened. You might describe her as being 'jolly hockey sticks'! Without turning her into a caricature, you can have fun with it. You will also notice the way the text is laid out as if it were verse. See if you can use

* Published in the volume *Arabian Nightmares* by Henry Naylor

the breaks in the line for emphasis, and to create space for her new thoughts.

- Tillie has left her home in Ipswich, Suffolk, in the hope of finding marriage to an Englishman who has been posted to a far-flung part of the British Empire. Such men were encouraged to marry girls sent out from England to prevent them from liaising and producing children with the 'natives'. In this sense, Tillie believes she is performing a duty and thereby satisfying 'Queen and Country'.

- What might the Lieutenant look and sound like? He is handsome and flirtatious. Perhaps you too have felt a similar attraction to someone based initially on their looks. See if you can picture him. You might like to base him on someone you know, or perhaps an actor you have seen in a film or play set at a similar time in history. I would suggest that you imitate his voice when he is talking to you.

- In comparison to the thrill of the handsome Lieutenant are the 'dullards' of Ipswich. How do you imagine Francis to look and speak? Again, you might like to base him on someone you know or a character from another story. It will be funny if you can imitate him too so that we get a sharp contrast between the two men.

- The speech is part of a much longer monologue, and Tillie is her own narrator. This section of the monologue comes at the very start of the play, and as you can see it goes backwards in time. You will need to make a clear break from describing the first meeting with the Lieutenant to what life is like back at home. So that when you say, 'Spinsters at twenty-five. My destiny', we know that you are not going to let that happen. Read the whole play to find out what happens to Tillie.

NB This play offers a number of other monologues from which to choose.

Tillie

❝ Three months at sea. The lump sugar is gone.
The eggs are rotten, and thrown overboard. India cannot
come too soon.
At dinner a handsome Lieutenant approaches. Winks
conspiratorially. And presents me with a fig. 'Slipped the
storemaster a few coins.'
I smile gratitude.
Then bite the flesh. There's a smell of rot, and the fizz of
ferment.
A maggot inside. Wrestling with its own being.
'Oh. Oh, I'm so sorry,' blushes the appalled Lieutenant.
He would crush it. But I stay his hand.
'It is one of God's creatures!… Insects. Hobby of mine – and
this one performs the most spectacular transformation in
nature. More wondrous than the caterpillar… Blind, now,
hopeless. But soon to grow wings, legs. Thousands of eyes.'
The Lieutenant snatches the fig, maggot and all, and crushes
it in a puffed fist. Red juice running through his fingers.
'Flies are not suitable discourse for a lady.'

[…]

I must confess.
I was a maggot, once, writhing on a dungheap called Ipswich.
Blind, wingless, directionless.
Thrashing around, trying to find a man. For my Christian
desire is to produce children for the Empire.
But there are no men in Ipswich. Only a succession of
squinting dullards…

My latest suitor is Francis, the pasty son of a leather
manufacturer.
A ninny, who has taken exception to the railways.
'Heed my words, these "railways" are but a fad. Some of these
vehicles travel in excess of twenty-five miles per hour.'
'Why is that so objectionable, sir?' I say.
He baulks. 'What lady is going to want to travel at such
ferocious speeds? Think of the damage to their hairstyles.'

'Ah, nullum bonum valebat perdere lapsas.'

'Er, quite,' he says.

I smirk. 'It means: "Never let an adventure get in the way of a good hairstyle".'

My father's jaw tense, as he bids Francis farewell.

'A capital woman,' says Francis, 'Capital. If only she hadn't floored me with her Greek.'

My father shuts the door, his rage, palpable.

'You are too spirited. How many men of means do you think there are in Ipswich?'

I look out on to the square. See the governesses wrapped in their threadbare gloves and carpet bags.

Spinsters at twenty-five.

My destiny. **99**

Epic Love and Pop Songs

Phoebe Eclair-Powell

TEN THINGS YOU NEED TO KNOW ABOUT DOLL:

- Doll is sixteen.

- She comes from an underprivileged background.

- Her appearance is rough because she doesn't take good care of herself, and her personal hygiene is not what it should be.

- She lives with her mum, who is permanently stressed out.

- Her dad left her mum for her mum's sister. So now her auntie is also her stepmother.

- Doll struggles to fit in. She is desperate to be popular, but she can be violent and people are scared of her.

- Doll says she is pregnant, but this is a lie. She has maintained the pretence by wearing a fake bump and taking pills to stop her periods.

- She hoped that telling people she was pregnant would get her some attention. But, if anything, it has made her situation worse. The other girls are competitive and hate the fact that Doll appears to have lost her virginity when they have been lying about losing theirs. In fact, she is still a virgin.

- Doll has one friend called Ted, who is a bit of a geek. Ted acknowledges that Doll can be violent: 'She did pull out a chunk of Samantha Hogan's hair', but tells us: 'I see something else, I see someone who needs looking after.'

- Doll is troubled. Her anti-social behaviour is a cry for help, and her tough outer shell is a cover for the hurt she feels inside.

FIVE THINGS TO HELP YOU PERFORM THE MONOLOGUE:

- Doll loves showing off. She craves attention, and this is her chance to shine. She is, cheeky, 'gobby' and a bit brash. It is a funny speech and you can have fun with it. (See note on talking to the audience in the introduction.)

- Think about the energy you will need to maintain. Doll is wired: her thoughts are like butterflies, flitting from one thing to the next. She is on a high, but be careful not to rush it.

- At this point in the play, we don't know that Doll is lying. You will have to convince us that what she says is true. The best way is to pretend that you really are pregnant and to think about an imaginary boyfriend who got you pregnant. You might like to try performing the speech with a fake bump, thinking of ways to disguise it before you reveal it. For instance, you could wear a baggy jumper that hides the bump and then take the jumper off to show the bump under a T-shirt that is closer fitting. Play around with it.

- Think about the other characters that she mentions. What do they look like? You will need a strong set of images in your head when you talk about your mum, dad, auntie and Ted.

- For all her bravado, Doll is immensely vulnerable. Be careful that she doesn't become a stereotype. Look for ways of finding the humour while still being connected to the sadness that she feels. The monologue is her way of making herself feel better.

NB This play offers a number of other monologues from which to choose.

Doll

❝ Hello, my name is Doll Evans and this is my show. And it is a one-woman show with supporting material – a backing dancer if you will – you know like one of them women that sing in a black dress at the back of the stage on *Britain's Got Talent* and wave their arms a bit – except my one's a man and he's called Ted Parker. But forget about him, because this is about me. And this is a list of things I like:
I like dunkin' biscuits in tea and then downing all the bitty bits in the bottom of the cup. I like watching *Dinner Date* on ITV3 because it reminds me that at least I'm not that much of a freak. I like wearing these pyjamas every night even though the towelling starts to smell of fanny really quickly, you know how it all rides up, well it does.

I go to Harris Academy and I'm in Year 10 don't ya know, yadda yadda I'm giving background, trust me it helps.

I'm really average is basically what I am trying to say,

I really, really am just that teenage girl you all know and won't sit next to on the back of the bus. That one. Music too loud brap brap I don't care, feet up on the seat, likes to link arms, laughs at everything and thinks 'you're well fit' is the best chat-up line ever. I'm her.

I live with my mum, cos well, that's the way it's always been, but my dad lives round the corner, with Auntie Cheryl who is both my aunt and my stepmum. Jezza Kyle ain't seen nuthin yet. Get me a double-page spread in *Take a Break*.

But no really it's fine. As my mum would say 'no really everyone I think you'll find IT'S FINE'. And then she chews on some more HRT and puts a nicotine patch on her nipple.

I think I'm what's pushing Mum over the edge at the moment to be honest.

Her blood pressure is well high and you can hear her teeth gnashing together in her sleep from my room. Except when she's like, crying.

I think it's because I'm pregnant.

Ta-dah.

I love a reveal don't you?

Trust me I'm not trying to be a bit-part in *Hollyoaks* it just sort of happened and then you think, 'well why not eh?' A little thing, round here, could be fun. I thought Mum would be more excited, she's always going on about me growing up and having nothing to live for blah blah, so now we both have something to live for – don't we?

I thought it was a great plan, but she was, well she was… I think it's cos I couldn't tell her who the father was. Sorry, but it's a secret – I might not even tell you guys. **"**

The Fall

James Fritz

TEN THINGS YOU NEED TO KNOW ABOUT TWO:

- The character known as Two is in her forties. However, the play was written to be performed by young people and so she can be played by someone your own age.

- She is married to a man known as One.

- They met when they were both young and have been together ever since.

- They have a son called Liam.

- They don't earn much money.

- They have always lived in rented accommodation.

- When One lost his job, Two got the idea that it would be good if they could sell his mother's flat to buy a place of their own. But One has never wanted to make his mother move out of her home.

- Two has never liked her mother-in-law.

- As Liam got older and they had more expenses, Two continued nagging One about selling the flat.

- When One's mother got so old and ill that she couldn't look after herself, Two suffocated her with a pillow.

FIVE THINGS TO HELP YOU PERFORM THE MONOLOGUE:

- Start by giving yourself a name. From what you know of her, what sort of person do you imagine Two to be? We know that she is pushy and selfish, although she would say that she is just looking out for her son. You must decide. See if you can fill in the gaps, using the opportunity to create a backstory and fully rounded character for yourself.

- She is talking to her husband, but she is not being honest when she says that her mother-in-law asked her to help her kill herself. Read the whole play to find out the truth. Whatever actually happened, it is clear that she has convinced herself that it was the right thing to do, and, that to avoid going to prison, it is vital she gets her husband to go along with her 'story'. Observe the way she repeatedly says 'I love you'. She knows she has done a terrible thing, but is desperate for him to forgive her/understand her.

- It is really important that you engage with the idea that life is financially so much harder for her generation than it was for her parents. With the rise in student loans and overall living costs perhaps you too can relate to this. Two is angry at the unfairness of it all, and to a certain extent she has good cause to feel this way.

- You will need to use your imagination to go from being angry at the unfairness of it all to actually murdering someone. It is an extreme situation. The great thing about plays is that they can present the 'what-ifs' in life so that the audience can be made to think about difficult subjects. The play especially written for people your age is a reminder that you too will be old and vulnerable one day, so you should think twice about the way you treat the elderly. See if you can really picture all that she describes from the pills to the pillow to the fact that she says it was gentle. She is probably lying about how easy it was, so see if you can play a little film in your mind's eye of how you would have *liked* it to be in order to *justify* what you have done. You could at the same time imagine a scenario where the killing was far from gentle. Like all liars she has managed to superimpose her version of events over the facts.

- The monologue has an interesting structure. You will see how many full stops and short sentences there are. If you observe these full stops and don't just run on to the next line, you can create a space for a new thought to pop into your head. Perhaps she is struggling. Perhaps it is an indication that she is lying, that she is running out of ideas or excuses. It certainly shows us just how hard she is having to work to get her husband on side.

Two

" Maybe you should sit down. [...]

It's not what you think so [...]

No listen. [...]

No!

Well.

I helped. [...]

She asked me. [...]

She asked me. To help her.
We were talking.
She didn't want to
Move
And
Since her fall
The pain
And
Our situation
Her flat
Those sharks
She knew
That this was best
So she asked me.
I'm sorry.
I love you.
For us.
For Liam.
Her flat.
It's meant for you.
Always.
That's what she said.
She asked me.
I'm tired she said.
I'm ready.
I said no

But
She kept asking
And.
I love you. [...]

Pills.
And I put a pillow
Resting on her.
I love you.
She didn't fight.
It was gentle.
I promise.
She knew.
Every year in that home
Would've been
Worse for her.
Worse for us.
Worse for Liam.
Worse for Liam.
I love you.
So.
Since her fall.
So much pain
And
She said

Eskimos. [...]

When Eskimos get old they walk out into the snow and die.
Choose their time.
And I thought.
If I was her.
What would I want? [...]

It was very brave. [...]

She asked me.
I love you.
Please.
She asked me. [...]

This flat. Her flat. We've got nothing else.
It's a life raft.

I loved her.
She was a good woman.
Had a good life.
But we couldn't afford.

This had to happen.
For Liam.
You understand that don't you?

You can hate me if you want. For the rest of our lives you can
hate me.
But think about him. He's what's important.
Not us. Not your mum.

She asked me to do it.
I need you to believe that.
For all our sakes.
Do you believe that? **"**

Fast*

Fin Kennedy

TEN THINGS YOU NEED TO KNOW ABOUT CARA:

- Cara is sixteen.

- She lives on a farm on the outskirts of a town.

- She 'rocks a sort of rural hippy look'.

- She lives with her mum who is into spiritual healing and yoga retreats, and her older sister Kirsty.

- Both Cara and Kirsty want to go to university.

- Cara's dad was a farmer.

- Their farm was an old-fashioned and traditional farm, and could not compete with the increase in industrial farming that was threatening their profits.

- Twelve months ago, Cara's father committed suicide.

- Cara discovered letters he had written to all the major supermarkets blaming them for driving him into debt.

- Since he died, Cara has lost her appetite. Her teachers are particularly worried about how grief is affecting her physically.

FIVE THINGS TO HELP YOU PERFORM THE MONOLOGUE:

- Since discovering her father's letters, Cara has become increasingly politicised about animal welfare and mass food production. Perhaps you share Cara's views or are passionate about another kind of cause. See if you can tap into this sense of injustice that drives the speech.

- Grief affects people in many different ways. Cara is angry about what happened to her dad, and also angry at her dad

* Published in the volume *The Domino Effect and Other Plays for Teenagers* by Fin Kennedy

for having left her. Without shouting, connect to this rage that she feels at her personal loss. It is at the root of her wider political views.

- Cara's friend Chris is recording Cara's speech on his phone. He is described as a 'vegan, eco-activist' and is very much on Cara's side. Think about what he might look like.

- If you don't already know about it, do some research into animal welfare – things like battery farms and fair trade – to discover what it is that Cara is objecting to. Really think about the snack machines and fast-food outlets. How do they smell? What does the food taste like? How do you feel after you've eaten crisps, chocolate and takeaway food? Cara is convinced that these things kill. (When one of Cara's classmates who likes this kind of food is diagnosed with diabetes, Cara's mission becomes increasingly real.)

- Think about the courage that Cara must have to want to meet with all the heads of the supermarket chains. Most sixteen-year-olds would be intimidated, but not her. See if you can connect to this feeling of strength, and play the monologue with confidence.

Cara

❝ Get your phone out. […] I want you to film me. […] (It's) A new campaign. I think you'll like it. […] Just hit record. […]

(*To camera.*) My name is Cara Leary. I'm in Year Eleven at Redford Secondary. Twenty-four hours ago I stopped eating. It was a sponsored fast for Oxfam, but I've decided to make it last. Twelve months ago, my dad lay down on some train tracks in the middle of the night. He was a farmer. For years he'd been screwed by the big supermarkets and fast-food chains who refused to pay him a proper price for his crops.

My dad was a quiet man, and never spoke about this. But I'm not quiet. And this is my protest. I will not be eating again until Redford Secondary bans all snack machines on school premises. I will not be eating again until Redford Secondary uses only fairly traded UK produce in its canteen. I will not eat again until our local council clamps down on the thirty-seven fast-food outlets that exist within one square mile of our school. And I will not eat again until I get meetings with heads of all the major supermarket chains which have an outlet in our town. This fast started for charity. But charity begins at home. Join me, and help demand a living wage for UK farmers and their families. Enough is enough. The revolution starts here. 🟄🟄

Folk

Tom Wells

TEN THINGS YOU NEED TO KNOW ABOUT KAYLEIGH:

- Kayleigh is fifteen years old.

- She comes from a small seaside town called Withernsea on the east Yorkshire coast.

- She is called Kayleigh because the name is pronounced the same as a 'ceilidh', a type of country dance, which is where her parents first met.

- Her mother died of cancer, and her dad left when she was little.

- She lives with her stepdad Trev, but they don't get on.

- Kayleigh is pregnant by a young man called Jason. He already had a girlfriend, but slept with Kayleigh anyway.

- Jason died recently, so Kayleigh, once again, is grieving someone close to her.

- Kayleigh has stopped going to school, but nobody in the school seems to care.

- She is sad and lonely and a little bit rough, but also kind, funny and thoughtful.

- Kayleigh has made friends with two older people – Winnie, a nun, and Stephen, who works in a local factory. The three of them meet in Winnie's house and sing folk songs together.

FIVE THINGS TO HELP YOU PERFORM THE MONOLOGUE:

- Today Winnie and Stephen have been arguing. Winnie is about to go on holiday and won't see Stephen for a while. Kayleigh is urging them not to fight. Winnie and Stephen have become like family to Kayleigh, which is why she hates them fighting. Imagine what they look like, so that when you are talking to them you can believe they are real people.

- Have a picture in your head of what Kayleigh's mum must have looked like, and imagine what sort of man Jason was.

- Kayleigh is young to have experienced the death of two people so close to her. It has made her wise beyond her years. Maybe it explains how she, the 'child', is telling the grown-ups how to behave.

- Because Kayleigh is pregnant, she is feeling sensitive. With the baby inside her she really needs things to be happy and calm.

- Winnie has a heart problem and is very ill. This, and the fact that Winnie is going away, makes it doubly important that they all stay friends.

Kayleigh

❝ You shouldn't be cross if you're not seeing each other for a bit.

That's what I think anyway. [...]

Especially cos, you know.

Cos you just never know, do you? Is the thing.

Like I remember with my mum, once I knew she was ill like not-getting-better ill I just got sort of obsessed with never falling out with her. To the point where it was weird and a bit strained and she had to have this chat with me, sort of reassuring me that if we'd had cross words or something and then I didn't see her again before she died she still definitely knew that I loved her. Dunno why, she just said it. But then we never fell out any more after that so. Job done.

And like, a lot of the time now when I'm thinking about Jason and that, cos I'm thinking about him quite a lot at the moment, we did not have that thing where we sort of parted nicely, like I think he just called me a slag or something and then I cried and told him his dick was a weird shape, which it wasn't actually, it was a lovely shape, but that is literally how we left it. And I regret that really, cos now he's dead and that, but I've got like his little son or daughter growing inside me. So probably it is best to just be nice to each other. Just like sort of in case. **❞**

Girls Like That

Evan Placey

THREE THINGS YOU NEED TO KNOW ABOUT GIRL WITH SHOULDER PADS:

- The girl with shoulder pad's only appearance is in this monologue. Use the opportunity to create for yourself a fully rounded character. You can start by giving her a name.

- The year is 1985 and the play has gone back in time. We later discover that the girl (aged between sixteen and eighteen here) is the mother of one of the play's present day characters.

- The girl is super bright, ambitious and ballsy. When she grows up she will become one of the most successful female chief executives of her generation.

FIVE THINGS TO HELP YOU PERFORM THE MONOLOGUE:

- You will need to research all the references from the time. 'Olivia' is Olivia Newton-John. You may have seen her in the film version of *Grease*. She was also famous for a song called 'Physical', and in the video she is exercising in Lycra. Consider also that there is limited technology (emails are a thing of the future), which is why the girl is having to deliver so many documents by hand. A Commodore 64 was a very early computer. When you see images of it now you realise just how bulky it was compared to modern computers, laptops and tablets, etc. Make sure you listen to the song 'Maneater' by Hall & Oates. You can watch the video online. Then follow the stage directions where she sings the last two lines of the third verse, 'Ooh the beauty is there, but a beast is in the heart', and the first two lines of the chorus, 'Oh oh here she comes, watch out boy'.

- Think about what you will wear. (See note on what to wear in the introduction.) Shoulder pads were a big thing in the 1980s when it was all about 'power-dressing'. The girl is very proud of her new outfit. We know she wears a skirt and assume that she has a fitted jacket or blouse with shoulder pads on top. The incident happened earlier that afternoon, so dress the part. If you are practising the monologue in jeans or leggings, be aware of how different you feel when you wear something smart. Without question it will bring you closer to the character and their situation.

- Her accent needs to be middle class. She comes from a privileged background and we know that 'Mummy' has contacts.

- Make a clear distinction in your mind between the girls at school and the girls who are also working at the law firm. When you refer to 'the girls' only, make sure you are clear which is which. In both cases the girl with shoulder pads struggles to make herself popular. What does this say about female friendship, solidarity and competition?

- What or who do you imagine Stanley to look like? I would suggest basing him on someone you know or have seen who is similarly lecherous. Enjoy getting the better of him. Notice the way she doesn't need to tell her mother about what happened. She can deal with these kind of men and is highly independent.

NB This play offers a number of other monologues from which to choose.

Girl with Shoulder Pads

66 Olivia is singing let's get physical. When she kicks I kick, when she punches I punch. And the afternoon is replaying in my mind which only makes me kick higher and my forehead sweat harder and my heart pound faster. It is 1985 and soon girls will run the world. Just wait till I tell the girls at school.

I have only worked at Pierce, Richards and Stanley for a week. My mother is nervous. They don't normally take on girls as young as me, but I want to be a lawyer so my mum has made some calls and got me this after-school gig a couple hours a week. I am what you call a 'runner' at the law firm. And runner is not a euphemism. From four to six p.m. I run between floors delivering mail, delivering coffee, delivering photocopies, delivering staples and paperclips, delivering memos and faxes from other floors. Lucky for me Olivia has got me in shape, cos some of the other girls who are a bit – well they just can't work as fast as me. Which is why I don't think they like me very much. 'I'm raising expectations' one of them has told me. And we're supposed to stick together. But I can't help doing my job well, can I? I even bought a new outfit, just for work. *Work.* How cool am I? The girls are like what are you doing after school? 'Oh you know, I'm just going to work. To my law firm.'

And the girls tell me to stay out of Stanley's way. Stanley is his first name and his last name which is the dumbest thing I've ever heard. Unless the girls are just saying that to trick me, but I don't care. And then today I've got these papers I gotta deliver to Mr Stanley's secretary. Only she's on break so I knock on his door. The first thing he says is: 'That's a pretty outfit.' See, it's important to dress for success. That's what my mum says. I don't tell him this obviously. I just say: 'Thank you sir.' And this is where it gets really good. As I'm handing him his papers, he puts his hand on my waist and he says: 'What an efficient young woman you are. You'll be put to good use here.'

'I want to be a lawyer, sir.'

And his hand has subtly slid further down my waist.

'Well this will certainly be a good experience for you then,' he says.

'I thought so too,' I tell him. 'But I'm not so sure. See you're supposed to be this amazing lawyer, but you seem not to know about any kind of employment law.'

He doesn't understand.

'See this, right here, would be considered sexual harassment in the workplace. And you seem not to know that. Either that or you've assumed that because I'm wearing a pretty skirt that somehow means that's an invitation or I'm too young or naïve to know otherwise. Either way, if you don't remove your hand from my firmly toned arse right now I will scream this whole office down, and then I will recruit Pierce, or Richards to sue the pants off you, and then I will call your wife.'

Beat.

'I'm glad you like my skirt. I'll be sure to wear it again.'

On my way out I see his secretary is back. She pretends to be typing on her Commodore 64 but I can see she's smiling.

When my mother picks me up, she asks how work was. I tell her 'fine' and she doesn't ask anything more. I turn up the car radio, Hall & Oates are singing:

She sings the last two lines of the third verse, and the first two lines of the chorus of 'Maneater' by Hall & Oates.

Here she comes indeed. **"**

Glitter Punch*

Lucy Burke

TEN THINGS YOU NEED TO KNOW ABOUT MOLLY:

- Molly is sixteen.

- She comes from Salford, next to Manchester.

- She lives with her mum, two brothers and her mum's boyfriend, who she says is useless. She is also scared of him.

- She loves her mother, but they sometimes have blazing rows. One was so bad that Molly stayed out all night and slept in the bus shelter.

- Molly's dad left two years ago: she says it has left an emotional hole inside her.

- Molly has very low self-esteem. She describes herself as being 'shit with words'. She says she is not clever, and although she is the first person in her family to go to college, she is studying travel and tourism which, she thinks, doesn't really count.

- Molly smokes cigarettes, but she doesn't like to drink alcohol or take drugs.

- Molly is not sociable. She says she hates people, and loves sleep.

- Molly is in love with a teacher at her college called John. He is twenty-seven. He says he loves her too. Read the whole play to find out what happens to them.

- Molly is vulnerable.

FIVE THINGS TO HELP YOU PERFORM THE MONOLOGUE:

- Although John appears in the story, the play is essentially one long monologue, and there may be other sections you would like to perform. At the very start of the play Molly is reading from her diary, and this gives you a clue about the content and tone of the play. It is a useful theatrical convention because in

* Published in the volume *Plays from VAULT 3*

a diary entry you can be uninhibited and totally free to express your innermost thoughts and feelings.

- Virginity is such an emotive subject. The 'right' time to lose your virginity is so dependent on the experiences of other girls or young women in your peer group. The important thing to consider here is that Salford is one of the most disadvantaged areas in the UK, and has one of the highest rates of teenage pregnancy, which is why Molly, at sixteen, is relatively old to be a virgin and feels like a freak. If you cannot do a Salford/Manchester accent and still want to perform the monologue, it is vital that you transpose the play to a similar area and change all relevant place names accordingly.

- Just before Molly delivers the monologue she is in John's car and they have been kissing. She begins to get aroused and doesn't understand why she feels wet between her legs. John explains that she hasn't peed herself and asks her if she's ever done this kind of thing before. First she says 'Loads of times', but then straight away says, 'No.' When she gets to the line 'Sorry' at the end of the monologue, it's as if she has picked up her conversation with him. It is touching and sad that she has to apologise for her inexperience. Really allow that 'Sorry' to resonate. Consider also her use of words like 'embarrassing', 'hole', ' 'too small', 'hate', 'lose', 'lost', 'shit', which go to make up all the negative things she says about herself.

- The monologue has an urgency, as if she has interrupted the action to speak what's in her head. In theatrical terms, this is called an 'aside', a bit like in a film when a character steps out of the story and talks directly to camera. Make a decision about whether wanting to feel normal like everyone else is even more important than having sex with John because she likes him.

- You will need to have a very strong idea of what John looks and sounds like. We know he is from Chiswick in London and Molly considers him 'posh'. He is eleven years older than her, which to Molly is really flattering. Perhaps you can connect to the feeling of being attracted to a teacher at school or a much older man, but then how would it feel if your fantasies became a reality?

NB This play offers a number of other monologues from which to choose.

Molly

" When you're a virgin and you're sixteen and you're from Salford it's fucking embarrassing. It's like this massive thing that you've got to try and hide only it's not a thing it's like a 'not-thing' which is even trickier to hide, like how do you hide a 'not-thing'? It's like a hole in your life and you can work around it but there's no covering it up because there's nothing to cover. You feel like there's probably definitely something wrong with you which obviously there is I mean my tits are too small and I hate people so I don't know in what world I could have had sex before but I still feel, embarrassed. And different. Like the only sober person at a party or something when everyone else is smashed.

And I don't get why they say you 'lose' your virginity. Because you're not losing anything are you? Are you? You're gaining fucking normality that's how I see it. It's easy to lose something, lost my phone twice in one day last week, always lose my homework, pretty sure I lost my mind the day Dad left but losing my virginity? Not easy mate. Surely it's more about finding something? Finding someone. Who wants you, and who you want. And I think it's John. I do. And I want to tell him this but I'm just Molly and I'm shit with words and that and my tits are too small so I just whisper

Sorry.

And he's kissing me and touching my knickers again and he says

'Fuck'

And it hurts a bit at first. But after that it's not so bad and anyway I love kissing him and he's mine and I'm his and we're safe. **"**

Home

Nadia Fall

TEN THINGS YOU NEED TO KNOW ABOUT ASIAN YOUNG MUM:

- The play is a piece of verbatim theatre based on interviews, so Asian Young Mum is a real person.

- Asian Young Mum is described as 'a British-Bengali teenager'. Her family are originally from Bangladesh and she is most probably aged between seventeen and eighteen.

- Her family are Muslim and hold traditional values.

- She was born in south London.

- When she was fifteen, her father sent her back to Bangladesh, presumably to find a husband. However, when things didn't work out there, and she returned to London, her father considered her a failure.

- Back in London, Asian Young Mum was caught between traditional family expectations and the culture of the West. She rebelled by drinking alcohol, having sex with a boy and getting pregnant by him.

- She left her own family to live with her boyfriend's family, but both her boyfriend and his family were abusive to her and she miscarried her baby.

- She became pregnant again, and this time gave birth to a baby girl. Meanwhile her boyfriend went to prison on domestic abuse charges.

- Asian Young Mum is now living in a place called Target East, which is a hostel specifically for the young homeless. Her baby girl is nine months old.

- Her boyfriend has left prison, and she is scared what might happen if he tries to see her, especially if he is drunk.

FIVE THINGS TO HELP YOU PERFORM THE MONOLOGUE:

- Because Asian Young Mum is a real person, her identity has been protected. Use the opportunity to create a fully rounded character for yourself and start by giving her a name. From what you know of Asian Young Mum, what do you imagine she could be called?

- The language here is conversational, loose and more like an improvisation than a carefully structured text. Bear in mind that the characters are being interviewed and the script is made up of their responses. See if you can capture that ease of being in the moment, not planning what you will say but letting thoughts come to you as you go along. It should appear that Asian Young Mum is just chatting.

- Asian Young Mum is willing to talk about her life. Perhaps it is a relief for her to be able to share and confide in someone she can trust. See if you can imagine the 'interviewer', and the room or office in which the interview is taking place, so that you have a focus for the speech. Enjoy being able to offload and see if you can picture the interviewer's reactions.

- As soon as her baby girl was born, Asian Young Mum had a focus and a strong desire to protect herself and her child. It was at this point in her life that she thought 'enough is enough' and managed to free herself from her abusers. When you are performing the monologue you might like to think that, by telling your story so openly and honestly, you are helping other young women who are in a similar situation, giving them courage to break free. This determination to look after herself runs through the entire monologue. Safety and security are her top priority, so it will be useful to keep this thought alive.

- The monologue takes in a number of different people, locations, and even time frames. Be clear about what happened to you when and where, and use your imagination to picture all that she describes.

NB This play offers a number of other monologues for different character types.

Asian Young Mum

❝ So well what happened, I went Bangladesh for a year and eight months cos of my father, um, so I missed year eleven, I come back and to them it's like my father, it's never enough, no matter how good you are it's like, you gotta do more, you gotta cover more wanted to go out – I couldn't, but because I wanted to – I'm so bad in his eyes.

Then well it was, I was on a day out, I was telling my parents I'm going work – (*Laughs.*) and... got on the bus, met the father... on the bus... what a crazy meeting... and he was already drunk and we just got talking and we just clicked and to me that lifestyle it was just like – wow! You're drinking you're having fun – and I didn't have groups of friends that used to go out and drink cos I wasn't allowed out and the work lot is just – at work. So that was the first time I met someone, who's... you know doing their own thing, it was just like wow to me then he was like yeah, try a bit, tried it, loved the drink. (*Laughs.*)

I never been West End until I met him, took me there and it was just a new life to me and it was like... woah... so, we just went out and just seen the lights and everything... (*Laughs.*)

Yeah I was madly in love with him and to me it was, learning everything from him and having fun and I just wanted to be with him, I used to go and see him in prison um... obviously my parents didn't know anything about him in prison but...

[...]

There was a few issues um, domestic violence and stuff like that which got a bit out of hand... I think there was an incident outside where he did hit me in a DLR station and then he headbutted me and stuff and the police got involved and, this has happened several times before but I just never put a statement through and then at the time I just thought enough's enough...

[...]

His family didn't even call when she was born, they haven't asked how she was… I went through hell when I was living with his family, it was just me a slave there to be honest, just cook for fourteen people…

I used to wake up in the morning and I just used to look at an empty mirror basically, I just used to see through me like, I didn't feel as if I existed sometimes… you're in the house, you just can't see yourself, you just, you just feel as if that's your life and… it's gonna end there.

I was on depression tablets as well, the first miscarriage I had was due to domestic violence so to me it was, I felt as though something was taken from me so I always wanted a baby since.

I do allow him to come here yeah, but I will have to, because of her, that's one good thing about Target though… which is extremely good for me and especially security… umm… but he does come down, if he does come down, if I know he's drunk I wouldn't let him near me. **"**

Home

Nadia Fall

TEN THINGS YOU NEED TO KNOW ABOUT ERITREAN GIRL:

- The play is a piece of verbatim theatre based on interviews, so Eritrean Girl is a real person.

- Eritrean Girl is about nineteen.

- She is a Christian.

- She is a refugee from Eritrea in north-east Africa, where the religious persecution of Christians has forced her to flee.

- She has a baby daughter who is still in Eritrea.

- She was illegally smuggled to the UK in a lorry.

- During the dangerous journey from Africa to Europe, Eritrean Girl was sexually molested.

- When she finally arrived in London, she met a man from Somalia who helped her get accommodation. She also made friends with and received help from members of her local church.

- Her then flat was broken in to and she was made homeless yet again. For a month and a half she had no where permanent to stay.

- Eritrean Girl is now living in a place called Target East in East London, which is a hostel specifically for the young homeless.

- Eritrean Girl, is brave, resilient and proud.

FIVE THINGS TO HELP YOU PERFORM THE MONOLOGUE:

- Because Eritrean Girl is a real person, her identity has been protected. Use the opportunity to create a fully rounded character for yourself and start by giving her a name. From what you know of Eritrean Girl, what do you imagine she could be called?

- The language here is conversational, loose and more like an improvisation than a carefully structured text. Bear in mind that the characters are being interviewed and the script is made up of their responses. See if you can capture that ease of being in the moment, not planning what you will say but letting thoughts come to you as you go along. It should appear that Eritrean Girl is just chatting. You will, of course, need to play the speech with an east African accent, bearing in mind that her English is not fluent, and she struggles to make herself understood.

- Eritrean Girl is willing to talk about her experience. Perhaps it is a relief for her to be able to share and confide in someone she can trust. See if you can imagine the 'interviewer', and the room or office in which the interview is taking place, so that you have a focus for the speech. Enjoy being able to offload and see if you can picture the interviewer's reactions.

- Unless you are a refugee yourself, it will be hard to imagine the bravery and enormous sacrifice she has had to make to come to the UK. Take time to research the politics of Eritrea and the persecution of its Christian community. Perhaps it is her religious faith that has kept her so strong.

- The monologue takes in a number of different people, locations, and even time frames. Be clear about what happened to you when and where, and use your imagination to picture all that she describes.

NB This play offers a number of other monologues for different character types.

Eritrean Girl

" Can we go to the office? Thanks.

ERITREAN GIRL *and interviewer find an empty office.*

Er… because you know our country Eritrea.

There is, religion, because of my religion it's not possible to um… to be free and to worship in Jesus Christ so because of that I… came out from that place.

The government rule the country but this is about the religion our religion is different. If you maybe they found you when you worship on a place, they gonna come, the police come and took you to prison.

Umm… 2008. I left that country. From my country to Yemen from Yemen to France by plane and half of by boat. From France to here I came by, you know by lorry? You know lorry? They brought us to… lorry and we get in, eight people together.

Um… you know the France one is very hard, because you know the… the agent brought me to one of, some people he introduced me to them and this is your country people and you have to look after her and to bring her and they said… okay and four, three boys and… three boys and I, the man is, he left he gave me money, like, to eat and to… get the hotel for one night and… um… when we going together with those boys, two of them very I scared of them because they flirting, something to have me you know… to do… the one is okay… he doesn't show anything he's thinking about future and – oh my God… I'm gonna spend tonight… with who… with which one? And… I don't know them just he left me with someone and… they are my country people but I don't know… even they are boys… if they are girls I don't mind and when we go to hotel, they have two rooms and we are four: me and three others…

So… I was thinking to have my only… but how? Is not possible to sleep for three, they say two, two. Okay… (*Pause.*)

I got on my knees and I pray, which one is good man… that doesn't touch me… I just sit down and I think about all of them… and suddenly I feel… I feel one, something this good and… we pay the hotel yeah? I said to them, 'I'm gonna choose to sleep with one. Him.' They said, 'Okay, okay why don't you choose me? Why don't you choose us? Whhhy? Nnno! We don't leave him just to you?' And then one of them he lay down on the bed and said, 'Okay, I'm sleeping here. Come sleep.' I said, 'Can you go out please? Already I paid for this room, I say, can you please go to your room, you two go – they say oh my God how do you know he's very good man? Because they know him, he is their friend. How, how is she know he's good man? How?! They wondering but I feel inside…

Inside the lorry there is a place, you know, they know they put us something in something, and we sit down when the policeman come and when they… looking, they don't find and the car is passed.

[…]

The car is leave us one place, even we don't know this is London just, we me and one man, the guy who was in the car.

The car is leave us one place and we walking to another. We don't know anywhere. We don't know anywhere, we don't have anything.

Just we walking yeah. […]

Suddenly like miracle you know I found him I found one guy on the street Somalian guy. We know the Somalia face. So straight away when I see him, this is Somalia I have to go and ask him.

He was helpful man. He brought me 'okay come come come' and he brought me to go that is the office you can go tell them everything. We explain everything we get somewhere to stay that night everything.

Yeah that's miracle for me like miracle, how do you believe that? **99**

Little Baby Jesus

Arinzé Kene

TEN THINGS YOU NEED TO KNOW ABOUT JOANNE:

- Joanne is fifteen. She is mixed-race.

- She lives with her mother in a council house in inner-city London. It is a rough and sometimes violent place to grow up.

- Joanne is highly sensitive, but has to appear tough in order to survive.

- Joanne and her mother do not get on, and Joanne hates having to go home. Her mother suffers from depression and at this point in the play is in hospital.

- Joanne has a half-brother, but she doesn't speak to him.

- When she is not at school, Joanne works in a launderette.

- In the monologue that follows, Joanne is at a retreat for disturbed children. It is in the countryside in the north of England, and Joanne is enjoying the peace and quiet.

- One day when all the other kids are out, she meets Kehinde. He also comes from London, very close to where she lives. Kehinde had been to the retreat before, but, following the violent murder of his twin sister, he ran back there looking for solace.

- Joanne has kissed and had sex with other boys, but she is now in love with Kehinde.

- At this point in the play she is pregnant by a boy called Baker. Kehinde knows about this. Read the play to find out what happens to the baby.

FIVE THINGS TO HELP YOU PERFORM THE MONOLOGUE:

- Joanne is at a crossroads in her life. See if you can capture that sensation of knowing that you are growing up. Perhaps you have had a similar experience of suddenly feeling like you are a different person from the one you were before.

- It is something about Kehinde's tenderness that enables her to change and to mature. You will need to have a strong visual image of what Kehinde looks like. Odd as it sounds, think about how he smells, what he sounds like and how good he makes you feel.

- How might it feel to be pregnant by one man and yet to be in love with another? This must complicate Joanne's already conflicted feelings. However, the intensity she feels for Kehinde also focuses her.

- Despite her hard life, Joanne tries not to take herself too seriously. See if you can find the humour in the monologue. Although she is deeply in love, then shaken and upset, she manages to see the funny side of things.

- 'Cyclops Polyphemus' was a one-eyed monster or giant from ancient Greek mythology. Joanne may not be the best at school, but she is streetwise, and knows and remembers stuff that interests her.

NB This play offers a number of other monologues from which to choose.

Joanne

❝ That night, I couldn't sleep. Frankie next door was killing me with the noises, having finger-sex with herself. So I goes up the hall to Kehinde's cupboard-room, quieter there, innit. I stood outside it for about ten minutes. I was stuck. My feet were cemented. I wanted to go in but – […]

Kehinde must've felt my presence because he opened up slowly and peeked his head out. Either that or he could see my shadow underneath his door. […]

We laid in his small cot. And obviously I've jammed with boys before but Kehinde was on some different echelon. We were communicating on some next wavelength – dolphin frequency. He just starred at me for ages like – right in my eyes like he could see directly to my soul. Like he tapped a channel to my spirit. That's him though, he just looks at me and I'm liquidised – not even on no sexual ting – come like Cyclops Polyphemus the way he be watching me. Well, it felt like that anyway. That's when I clocked he was a blue magnet. Him blue and me red. The way we attracted was as if he already had a magnet vacancy. As if I was filling up a space that was once inhabited. See, just when I thought I had conquered the world of ferromagnetism, behold, Kehinde the blue magnet; cool on the outside and hot in the middle.

He combed his fingers through my hair. And he discovered the scar on my head – […]

And I remembered Mum. And he remembered someone. And a tear rolled down my cheek and onto his chest. And I used my finger as the pen, and my tears as the ink, to draw perfect circles on his chest as the canvas. And then a single kiss came down and landed on my head and it was suspended there for a while. He held me tight. And he said –

'Finally.'

(*Touched.*) *'Finally.'* He said *'Finally.'* About *me.* No one's ever waited for me before.

I never knew so many emotions could hit you at the same time. And the thought that there was no guarantee, no promise, that I would ever meet another soul who would hold me like he did that night, made my heart beat out of control like his own. Made my head explode. In that moment, I swear, I was forced to grow the fuck up. I said to myself –

(*In tears.*) *'Jodie. Nah nah. Joanne. You're not a little girl no more, y'understand. You gotta use this – (Points to head.) now. More crucial than ever. No, it hasn't been all roses but move – the fuck – on. You're a big girl. Fuck…'*

I was crying, boy. I don't cry. I never cry. But I was crying – real talk.

Then the following morning, Kehinde, 'the boy who never leaves', had to leave. Abruptly.

Boy.

I don't know what I got that's making them leave. If ever loved by a magnet like Kehinde you have been loved totally. This magnet will pry apart your ribs, ram its hand into your chest cavity, steal all of your heart, and leave the phattest scar 'cross your chest just so's you never forget.

I *could* tell you that him just suddenly leaving didn't take the piss out of my life completely, that it didn't leave me unbalanced, that it didn't relaunch misery. **99**

Little Gem

Elaine Murphy

TEN THINGS YOU NEED TO KNOW ABOUT AMBER:

- Amber is eighteen.

- She is an only child.

- She is from Dublin, the capital city of the Irish Republic.

- She has just recently left school and is working in a call centre.

- She has a boyfriend call Paul, but she is much more in to him than he is to her.

- Amber's father is a drug addict, but no longer lives with the family.

- Amber's mother Lorraine suffers from depression, and Amber finds it hard to get along with her.

- Amber is closer to her grandmother than to her mother. When she finds out that she is pregnant, she tells her grandmother first.

- Amber is very funny, but she is also very sad. It could be the case that she covers her sadness by cracking jokes the whole time.

- Amber is insecure, especially around men.

FIVE THINGS TO HELP YOU PERFORM THE MONOLOGUE:

- Imagine where you are. The speech starts off with Amber in the toilets where she works and then at her desk in the call centre.

- Amber is talking to the audience. (See note on talking to the audience in the introduction.) You will also need to get very strong images in your head about what the other characters might look and sound like.

- You will need to stay in the moment as she waits for the test results, and then for the realisation to sink in as she works out how it might have happened in the first place. See if you can chart this journey.

- On the one hand she would secretly like to be pregnant: 'If I was… Paul'd have to…', and on the other she is horrified at the prospect: 'We hardly made a baby outta that did we?' Decide to what extent she thinks this baby might bring her and Paul closer together.

- Have fun with the speech. Amber is very playful. She likes to entertain and does good impressions of people. Note the stage direction, 'She stretches out her arms and legs and flails about a bit'. See if you can find a bold physicality when describing this moment.

NB This play has several other monologues from which to choose.

Amber

66 In two minutes I'll get an 'accurate' reading. Imagine me being pregnant? Like, a ma. There's no way. Imagine Paul being a da! That's mad. Like, I know I've nothing to worry about but Mandy has my head doing fucking overtime. My yokes are always all over the place but… I actually can't remember when I got my last one. If I was… Paul'd have to… (*Looks at the strip.*) Oh my God, my heart. Negative. I knew it. Open the door; show Jo. The fucking relief. I knew it, but you know… Jo checks the box, then checks it again. She says it's positive. Give over, an 'X' means no. She turns it a bit and says: 'Plus means positive.' Bollix.

Sitting at my desk waiting for calls to come through. I'm on directory enquiries today for an English phone company. This fella rings in, looking for a cab firm in Hackney. He doesn't know the name of the place or the road it's on but it's definitely somewhere in Hackney, yeah… Do I not know it? How would I bleedin' know it? I'm about to start a search, but it feels too much like work and he's been real ignorant so I cut him off. Trying to remember when the fuck it could've happened cos in fairness we're always real careful. I've done three pregnancy tests and they all say the same thing.

There was this one night, when we got back to his gaff and I was wrecked. Was lying there waiting for the bed to stop spinning so I could climb aboard the night train. He was off somewhere – probably playing that fucking Xbox with Stee – then he comes in and starts nudging me.

'You awake? You awake? You awake?'

'Well, I am now.'

Was so knackered, did the starfish – you know – (*She stretches out her arms and legs and flails about a bit.*) decked out, no energy. He's going at it like a mad thing and I don't know… Must've nodded off – only for a minute, mind – cos then I heard – 'Oh shite, Amber, it's split! Amber! Amber! Amber!'

I'm like, 'What, what, what?'

'Were you asleep?' He says, disgusted.

'Nooo, I had me eyes closed cos I was getting really into it.'

'I might as well be into necrophilia.'

At that stage I could feel my headache starting so I just said: 'Fuck off.'

But the next day I said to me ma: 'Here, what does necrophilia mean?'

The look on her face was pure horror.

'What weird shit are you getting up?'

'Ah, nothing,' says I. 'Heard it on the telly.'

It must be really bad – like when they poo on ye or something. Maybe it's his posh way of saying I'm shite in the sack. He does that sometimes, uses big words I don't understand, bet the cunt doesn't know what it means either. We hardly made a baby outta that, did we? **99**

Mogadishu

Vivienne Franzmann

TEN THINGS YOU NEED TO KNOW ABOUT BECKY:

- Becky is fourteen.

- She lives with her mother, Amanda, and stepfather, Peter.

- She is an only child.

- Becky's real dad committed suicide when Becky was younger. He hanged himself with a tie that Becky had given him as a Christmas present.

- For a long time after that, Becky did not speak.

- Becky still suffers from depression and self-harms. She cuts herself to the point where her arms and legs are now a criss-cross of scars.

- Despite being down, Becky is also brave, funny and clever.

- Becky's mother is a teacher at Becky's school. She has been wrongly accused of racially abusing one of her pupils, and has been asked to remain at home while the case is being investigated. This has put a lot of pressure on the family, and Becky is not sleeping well.

- Becky's relationship with Peter has always been strained. He is not her real father and it is hard for her to accept him.

- Read the whole play to see what happens when Becky confronts the boy who is accusing her mother. It takes great courage for Becky to do so, and gives an insight into the strength of her character.

FIVE THINGS TO HELP YOU PERFORM THE MONOLOGUE:

- Becky is talking to her stepdad, Peter. Just before the monologue, Becky has asked Peter if he can remember what she was like when they first met. He tells her that she was sad and that she didn't speak for six months. Becky can't remember this, but her decision to start talking about the old pier and her father is her way of explaining *why*.

- Becky feels guilty. Although it is not the case, on some level she blames herself for her father's death. See if you can connect to this feeling. Even though you may not have experienced a tragedy like Becky's, you will most probably know what it is to have done something 'wrong' and to feel guilty about it.

- Becky and Peter are in the kitchen at breakfast. Becky has not slept well and is late for school. See if you can imagine the room. You may like to place Peter directly in front of you, as if you are sitting facing him across a table. Imagine what he looks like and what his reactions might be. Think about how on the one hand you want to distance yourself from him (he is not your real dad), but on the other you need his comfort and reassurance that you are not a bad person.

- Think about the significance of the photograph. It is as if the picture of the 'headless man' is prophetic or a kind of bad omen of what was to come.

- The speech is highly descriptive. Make sure that you are seeing everything she describes in your mind's eye. Get a strong image of the pier, the old lady, her red coat, her shaky hands, the cafe where they had tea, her house, etc. The more detail you can bring to these images, the more effective the monologue will be.

Becky

❝ Did you ever see the old pier in Brighton? […] My dad was obsessed by it. […] He was always going on about how it was deteriorating. He used to take a photo of it every week so he had a record of it falling down. What a weirdo. […] I've got this photo of me and him standing in front of it. This really old woman took it. Dad asked her to and she was shaking because she was nervous in case she took it wrong. He bought her a cup of tea after and he kept making her laugh calling her 'lady in red' and 'scarlet woman' because she had this red coat on. He could be really cheesy sometimes. I mean really fucking cheesy.

Pause.

And then we walked her back to her house and when we got there, she bent right down and took my hand and said, 'You're very lucky to have such a wonderful daddy.'

Pause.

Talk about cheesy. That is cheese on toast. That whole story is mature cheddar on a piece of poor–little–me toast. […] If I close my eyes, I can see that woman so clearly. I can remember everything about her. Everything.

Pause.

But when I think of Dad, I can't see him. It's like he's getting further and further away from me and the more I try, the more I try to imagine, the more I look at photos of him to try and remember, the stranger he looks. […] When we got the pictures back, she'd cut his head off. In the photo I'm holding hands with a headless man. **99**

Multitudes

John Hollingworth

TEN THINGS YOU NEED TO KNOW ABOUT QADIRA:

- Qadira is eighteen.

- She is a British Muslim of Pakistani heritage.

- She comes from Bradford in west Yorkshire.

- Her mother died a few years ago of bowel cancer.

- She lives with her dad, who is called Kash. Kash is a Tory councillor in Bradford and is standing for election as an MP.

- Kash has a white girlfriend called Natalie. Qadira hates her.

- Qadira has been brought up in a secular and liberal environment.

- Qadira is angry at the repeated attacks on Muslim countries around the world, and the rise of racism in the UK. What is more, she is fed up with talking about these issues and now wants to take direct action.

- A women's peace camp has been set up in the city to protest against Western interventions in the Middle East, and Qadira has become radicalised.

- Qadira has been experimenting with wearing niqab, which covers her entire head and face, leaving only her eyes visable.

FIVE THINGS TO HELP YOU PERFORM THE MONOLOGUE:

- Qadira has arranged to meet the 'sister', one of a secret band of Muslim women who groom other young Muslim women to perform acts of violence. The monologue is made up of their conversation in which the 'sister' is largely silent. I have given Qadira a few of her lines for clarification. You will need to imagine the sister telling Qadira that it isn't a test, ordering Qadira to open the bag, and instructing her to burn what's inside before you 'repeat back' what you have heard.

- It would be good to perform the monologue with a big rucksack in front of you. What the audience don't know, but you do, is that there is a Union flag inside there. The 'sister' wants Qadira to burn it while her father is making an important speech at the Conservative Party Conference. Read the whole play to find out what happens when she sets fire to the flag.

- It is important to remember that Qadira is essentially a good person, trying to do the right thing. As she says in the monologue, she is scared and doesn't want to hurt anyone, least of all herself.

- As soon as she is given the rucksack she tries to backtrack. See if you can chart her varying excuses from not wanting to blow herself up to using the death of her mother as an explanation for her reluctance. Work hard to convince the 'sister' to let you go. What is more, the 'sister' is wearing jilbab, which covers the entire body, and niqab, so it makes sense that Qadira would not be able to identify her. Perhaps you too have been in a situation that felt like a good idea at the time, but then became too much for you? How does it feel to be in too deep? It may not be as extreme as this, but see if you can connect to that feeling of changing your mind, sensing danger and having made a big mistake.

- See if you can really capture that moment of realisation that it is only a flag that she wants you to burn. The contrast from terror to relief is really marked in the speech, and it is important that you make this shift. I would recommend putting a flag in the rucksack so that when you go to look you don't have to pretend seeing it. Out of context, you could even lift it up so that the audience get a better idea of what it is she wants you to do. Try both ways and see which one you prefer.

Qadira

❝ Are you going to say anything at all?

[...]

Right.

[...]

Is it a – ?

[...]

Is it?

[...]

Is this a test?

[...]

Do you know? If it is or it isn't? Or are you just the person who drops it off?

[...]

Okay. So maybe you put it together. Want to make sure it's used properly. Fair enough. But I'm not blowing myself up – no way – seriously – I never said I'd do that – that was never part of the plan so if you want me to do that then I'm sorry but you'll have to look elsewhere.

[...]

Look. I was just sick of talking. *Talking* and doing *nothing*.

[...]

This *is* a test isn't it? Whether I'm ready to put myself on the line. Whether I can *do* this.

[...]

What? *Shit*.

[...]

Look. Can I just go? I mean I haven't seen your face. Barely heard your *voice* and – . And I mean. Your skin looks. Sort of. Average colour. Not being – . But it's not like I could pick you

out of a police line-up or anything. Not that I'd go to the
police or anything. I wouldn't do *that*. It's just. I mean. D'you
know what? My mum – died. Actually. Y'know? Bowel cancer.
It's a few years now but – . Well I've been a bit – . Been quite
– . I'm just a kid. That's what they said. The others – in the
group. Said I wasn't ready. So can I just – go? Cos I'm
actually. Quite scared. So – . If it's okay... I'll just –

[...]

Sorry?

[...]

Right. But – .

[...]

I mean it's not going to *do* anything, right? Not *here*. Not in
Pudsey train station. You and me and a couple of *pigeons*.

[...]

Right. Yep. Doing it now.

Gingerly approaches the bag. Opens it.

What – is that...?

She explores it carefully. [...]

What – is that *it*?

[...]

Burn it?

[...]

Right.

[...]

So, there's not a – ?

[...]

Well why didn't you say?... *Freaking me out!* I mean – And it's
just a – . I thought it was a – . And I was – . Sorry. About –
that. Before. I thought I had to – . But anyway. I mean – this.
Yeah. *This* I can cope with. **99**

My Name is Rachel Corrie

Taken from the writings of Rachel Corrie
Edited by Alan Rickman and Katherine Viner

TEN THINGS YOU NEED TO KNOW ABOUT RACHEL:

- Rachel Corrie was a real person.

- She died on 16 March 2003, whilst attempting to protect a Palestinian home that was being flattened by an Israeli bulldozer.

- Although she was twenty-three when she left home to join the International Solidarity Movement in Gaza, at this point in the timeline of the play she is still a teenager.

- Rachel is from Olympia, Washington, in America.

- Her family (she has a brother and sister) are comfortably off.

- She is extraordinarily brave. The fact that she was prepared to die for what she believed in shows us this.

- From an early age Rachel was politicised. She held strong and passionate views about human rights.

- A school trip to Russia is a seminal experience. It is after this that she develops her 'wanderlust'.

- Read the whole play to understand her unique voice. The story is one long monologue, made up of extracts from her journals and emails. It gives a great insight into her personality and why she felt the need to help those less fortunate than herself.

- Beyond this you will need to familiarise yourself with the Israeli/Palestinian conflict. The arguments are hugely complex and, as it was for Rachel, far from easy to understand.

FIVE THINGS TO HELP YOU PERFORM THE MONOLOGUE:

- Rachel likes to identify herself as the 'outsider'. She explains this sense of being different from her peers as having 'fire in my belly'. See if you can capture this rebellious spirit.

- Rachel is restless. She craves experiences that are out of the ordinary, and this forms the basis of the monologue. She is eager to explain this to us as it will inform her later actions.

- Rachel became increasingly troubled by mainstream American culture and politics. Take time to think about what in particular was offensive to her about the narrowness of her life back home. Was it the lack of adventure? The fact that everything is so clean, neat and tidy? Or, American 'Isolationism' and general lack of interest in the outside world?

- The monologue is highly descriptive. See if you can imagine all that she describes. The more detailed you can make these pictures in your mind, the more you will be able to transport us. Take, for example, the line 'the coal dust on the snow'. The more you can visualise the black against the white the better.

- The speech is full of contrasts. Let these 'on the one hand this, and, on the other hand that' phrases drive the speech. Think about the fact that the very *dirtiness* of Russia was *beautiful* to Rachel while, by the same token, the natural *beauty* of where she lives in America ultimately leaves her feeling *empty*.

NB This play offers a number of other monologues from which to choose.

Rachel

66 Okay. I'm Rachel. Sometimes I wear ripped blue jeans. Sometimes I wear polyester. Sometimes I take off all my clothes and swim naked at the beach. I don't believe in fate but my astrological sign is Aries, the ram, and my sign on the Chinese zodiac is the sheep, and the name Rachel means sheep but I've got a fire in my belly. It used to be such a big loud blazing fire that I couldn't hear anybody else over it. So I talked a lot and I didn't listen too much. Then I went to middle school where you gotta be *cool* and you gotta be *strong* and *tough*, and I tried real hard to be cool. But luckily, luckily I happened to get a free trip to Russia and I saw another country for the first time.

In the streets and the alleys it was an obstacle course of garbage and mud and graffiti. There was coal dust on the snow, everything was dirty. And they always said to us, 'How do you like our dirty city?' Oh, but it was so pretty with the little lights in the windows and the red dusk-light on the buildings. It was flawed, dirty, broken and gorgeous.

I looked backwards across the Pacific Ocean and from that distance some things back here in Olympia, Washington, USA seemed a little weird and disconcerting. But I was awake in Russia. I was awake for the first time with bug-eyes and a grin.

On the flight home from Anchorage to Seattle everything was dark. Then the sun began to rise, the water was shining, and I realised we were flying over Puget Sound. Soon we could see islands in that water, evergreen trees on those islands.

And I began to sob. I sobbed in all that radiance, in the midst of the most glorious sunrise I'd ever seen, because it wasn't enough. It wasn't enough to make me glad to be home. **99**

Natives

Glenn Waldron

TEN THINGS YOU NEED TO KNOW ABOUT a.:

- Today is her fourteenth birthday.

- She comes from a very wealthy family. They have servants.

- She lives on a small clean island somewhere in the Indian Ocean. It is the kind of place where people pay very little tax.

- She goes to an expensive international school.

- Her parents work abroad and she very rarely sees them. As far as we know, she is an only child. This probably makes her feel doubly lonely.

- Like many rich kids she is materially wealthy, but poor in love and affection.

- Her friends are similarly wealthy. They all lead very sheltered lives.

- Despite their level of education, their day-to-day values are shallow, and their lives are completely dominated by social media.

- Her precise heritage or ethnicity is unspecified, so she can be played by someone who looks like you!

- Despite the peer pressure, she is surprisingly individual. When you read the whole play you will see that she has the potential to break free from the crowd.

FIVE THINGS TO HELP YOU PERFORM THE MONOLOGUE:

- Give yourself a name. Although the playwright calls her 'a.' it will help you to understand/feel closer to her if you know what she is called.

- Think about her accent and the way she speaks. Although she can be played by any nationality, it is important that you capture the fact that she is a 'rich kid'. You might like to try what is known as a Mid-Atlantic accent. This is somewhere between English and American, and is typical of people who attend international schools.

- See if you can imagine what Lily Kwok, Suki Newhouse, Brooke, Amber and all the other girls that she mentions look like.

- Get a very clear picture in your head of the 'pistachio-green velvet banquette' and what it would look like inside a Miu Miu shop. If you don't already know, take time to look up what sort of clothes they sell.

- At this point in the play, she is feeling confident within the group. What sort of pressure does this need to be 'perfect' have on her? Read the whole play to see what happens when the pressure gets too much.

NB This play offers a number of other monologues from which to choose.

a.

❝ It's the morning of Lily Kwok's Funky Fourteenth Birthday Dance and I'm sat in Miu Miu.

I'm looking at things on my phone while I wait for Amber.

I'm sat on the pistachio-green velvet banquette you always sit on in Miu Miu, taking small sips of the Lime Cucumber Juleps they always give you in Miu Miu.

And – and I live on a small, clean island with a twenty-per-cent tax ceiling and eighty-four-per-cent humidity, floating somewhere in the Indian Ocean.

[…]

I'm looking at things on my phone and also counting.

Counting the seconds between sips of the Lime Cucumber Julep.

Because there's a perfect number.

Because Suki Newhouse read in *Vogue* that the optimal ingestion rate for liquids is exactly one sip per thirteen seconds and that's the perfect number.

[…]

And I'm counting the sips but also looking at the feed on my phone.

I'm going through all the pictures and videos everyone has posted in the last forty-six seconds.

Everyone at the Orchard Hills All-Girls Academy for Academic Excellence.

(That's my school.)

And I'm looking at this picture Bettina Rice-Peters has posted and I really can't decide.

I'm really, like, not sure.

Whether it's worth five hearts or six.

It's this close-up of a Smoky Egyptian Cat's-Eye she's tried for Lily Kwok's Funky Fourteenth Birthday Dance and it's not a seven. It's definitely not a seven!

It's a little scrappy around the waterline and the line should, like, kick out at the end not just swoop and it's definitely not a seven.

And Annika Albrecht did a Smoky Egyptian Cat's-Eye last week with a perfect kick.

And she had an aggregate score of five-point-nine.

So how can this be a six?!

[…]

I take it back and give her six hearts.

Because the swoop is actually quite kicky.

And Jennifer Cheng Khoo's given her four.

Which is so, like, harsh.

Just really – *harsh*.

And then I'm, like, scrolling through my feed and I'm looking at a video that Mia Ferrero has just shared.

This video of her fact-finding trip to the West Bank last weekend for history class.

And even though I'm fundamentally in favour of Mia's proposed two-state solution, unlike Christy Vanderbilt and Jennifer Cheng Khoo who are, like, so *Zionist* in outlook, I think the film is essentially a little reductive in its argument and I give it seven hearts.

And then I'm looking at this video that Summer Klatten-Smith has posted of her new pug. And I'm giving it a full nine hearts (minus one for respiratory issues) when I get a message from Brooke.

Brooke who's also waiting for Amber.

Brooke who has two hundred and thirty-six more followers than me and three hundred and seventy-eight more followers than Amber and also once held a python in *Teen Vogue*.

Brooke who thinks Amber is Literally Taking Forever.

That's what the text from Brooke says: 'Amber is Literally Taking Forever.'

Five exclamation marks four smiley faces one kiss.

And I text back straight away.

'God, I know.'

'Tell me about it, babes.'

Three eye-rolls two egg timers one kiss.

And then there's a bleep and I check my phone but it's not mine.

It's actually Brooke's.

Brooke who is… sat there right next to me on the pistachio-green velvet banquette in Miu Miu.

Brooke who checks her phone and smiles. Or smiles as much as Brooke does.

And then the store's sending over a sales representative with more Lime Cucumber Juleps.

And she's asking us all these questions.

Questions about Lily Kwok's Funky Fourteenth Birthday Dance (because, like, everyone on this island knows about Lily Kwok's Funky Fourteenth Birthday Dance).

And as we answer the questions, she's nodding and laughing.

Even though what we're saying isn't necessarily – funny?

And then she's asking Brooke 'What's your favourite song to dance to?'

And at this, Brooke and I just burst out laughing.

Which is not a particularly cool thing to do in the face of the sales representative in Miu Miu.

But we can't help it, the bursting-out laughing, we really can't!

Because – no one actually dances at Lily Kwok's Funky Fourteenth Birthday Dance.

No one would ever dance at Lily Kwok's Funky Fourteenth Birthday Dance.

That just isn't a thing that could – happen.

And the idea of it is just crazy.

It's crazy! **99**

One For Sorrow

Cordelia Lynn

This play deals with adult themes. It has content and language that some readers might find disturbing or offensive.

TEN THINGS YOU NEED TO KNOW ABOUT CHLOE:

- Chloe is in her late teens.

- She comes from a privileged background.

- She lives in a big house in London with her parents and older sister Imogen.

- She goes to an independent school.

- She is studying A-level Art.

- She has a fascination for all things violent and destructive, which she expresses through her artwork.

- She is sexually active, and has an ex-boyfriend called Freddie.

- She is provocative, and swears a lot.

- She is precocious, often arrogant and thinks she knows more than she does.

- Her parents are worried about her behaviour and her state of mind.

FIVE THINGS TO HELP YOU PERFORM THE MONOLOGUE:

- Chloe is talking to John. He is a young British Asian man, whom her sister has invited into the house during a terrorist attack on the streets of London. He is a complete stranger.

- Chloe fancies John. See if you can imagine what he looks like. She is obviously trying to impress him. Notice the way she makes it clear to John that a) she is sexually active, and b) she dumped her boyfriend, so is now single. Decide to what extent this is by way of a come-on to John.

- Despite the atrocity of the night's events, and the increasing number of casualties being reported on TV, Chloe is excited by the violence. See if you can let this thrill at what is happening on the outside feed into her desire for John inside her own home.

- You will need to imagine what Freddie looks like. It would be helpful to make him totally different from John, and weaker in every way. An avatar is a virtual image and therefore something not real. Unlike John, who appears full of depth to Chloe, Freddie is shallow.

- Chloe speaks quickly as if her thoughts just tumble from her head. Without rushing the speech, see if you can stay on top of her thoughts, which, as far as she is concerned, are very important. Notice how long some of her sentences are before a full stop finally completes her train of thought.

Chloe

❝ I've been thinking about this thing, right, and as an example, my ex, Freddie, he was really great in some ways, but

[…] for example, he'd say he was a feminist and stuff but actually I don't think he was because when there was food or something he'd always give himself a bigger portion than me and I think that's probably quite a male thing to do, I mean, hashtag Not All Men, but I don't think most women would do that and the fact is in the end I just didn't find him sexually attractive because – […]

Well

it was sort of like

there was nothing there. Like it looked like he knew how to talk the talk and even walk the walk, but I actually don't think he believed it, any of it, and the thing is it's not his fault because we all look like we know how to walk the walk and talk the talk like, for example, my school's totally in to Intersectionalism now because Immy came back from university and was like

Intersectionalism

so I went into school and was like,

Guys, my feminism will be intersectional or it will be bullshit

and everyone was like, Yeah, my feminism will be intersectional or it will be bullshit but actually I go to this private school and I swear there are only like three black people there and that's not very intersectional or at least diverse and then recently my friend got into this argument with one of the black girls about what Intersectionalism is and afterwards I suddenly thought that it might not be okay to argue with a black girl about what Intersectionalism is if you're white but I just don't know.

[...] And I don't mean to be too down on everything because it's still really amazing in some ways if you think that when Immy was at school there wasn't even any feminism at all, except for weird girls with no friends like Immy [...] But to get back to Freddie sometimes I just don't see the point in him existing. [...] Because we had this argument where I was saying I could understand why these men do the bad things, I mean the terrorists and the ones that go to fight. Because actually their worlds have been destroyed, by us, it's true, and their homes and their families and everything and it's like, of course they want to fight! Wouldn't you want to fight? And even the ones from this country – [...] Well, I'm just saying, there's so much racism and stuff so of course they're angry and they want to do something, they want to fight, and I was telling Freddie I could understand that. I understand how they feel. And actually, if I were them, I'd fight too.

And Freddie was like, No way, He would never, How could I even say that, and suddenly I just felt cold inside, and suddenly I found myself thinking, Well what would you do?

Really?

I mean who are you, what do you really believe? I don't believe you really believe in anything at all. And you're just walking around saying all the right stuff but inside. There's nothing there. Like he's just a

I don't know.

Like an avatar.

And the cold inside was this chill of realising that I'm fucking an avatar.

An avatar for…

What? A decent modern man?

But it's easy to be a decent modern man, isn't it? Whereas it's much harder to actually

engage

or.

And it's like there's all this stuff happening and I'm just here making Art for my A levels and thinking about art school because that's just this acceptable way for me to engage but actually if I were them I would want to engage properly. Like really engage. I would want to fight. And it scares me but I think I actually would. And what scares me most of all is I think there's a part of me now that's trying to make this imaginative leap, to –

A part of me that's trying to imagine whether I could go and fight all the same. I mean despite everything. I mean –

That's all I'm trying to say.

What do you think?

What do you think, John?

John? **"**

Pandas

Rona Munro

TEN THINGS YOU NEED TO KNOW ABOUT LIN HAN:

- Lin Han is nineteen.

- She is Chinese.

- Her native language is Mandarin.

- Lin Han works for a rug distribution company that is based in China.

- She has travelled from China to Edinburgh in Scotland in order to do business with a company that wants to import Chinese goods.

- Over an eighteen-month period and before she arrived, she exchanged emails and images with Jie Hui, a young Chinese man who works for the British distribution firm.

- During that time, Lin Han fell in love with Jie Hui, and when she arrived in the UK she had hoped that he would feel the same.

- Jie Hui has told Lin Han that he cannot feel the same. That despite the emails and images, he hardly knows her, that it is too soon for them to start a relationship and that she should slow down.

- When Jie Hui's business partner is shot by his ex-girlfriend, Lin Han mistakenly thinks that it was Jie Hui who tried to kill him.

- In the monologue that follows, Lin Han has rushed to the police station accusing Jie Hui of murder.

FIVE THINGS TO HELP YOU PERFORM THE MONOLOGUE:

- Although the speech is in English, Lin Han is actually speaking in Mandarin Chinese. You don't therefore need to speak with a heavy Chinese accent or in broken English.

- Lin Han is conflicted. On the one hand, she is desperately in love with Jie Hui and would normally do anything she could to protect him, and on the other she is convinced that he is a murderer and feels an obligation to report him. Perhaps you too are or have been conflicted about someone you like or love. Although your situation may not have been so extreme, perhaps you have been attracted to someone who you know to be a liar or unkind in some way. See if you can capture her confusion.

- Make sure you can imagine what Jie Hui looks like. Paint a picture in your mind and make him as attractive to you as possible so that you can connect to the strength of her passion.

- Although Lin Han has come to report the attempted murder, she spends most of her time talking about her feelings for Jie Hui. People who are in love often feel the need to talk and share in this way. Consider also the loneliness she is experiencing, but here, with the police officer and interpreter, she has at least an opportunity to speak to someone and to get it off her chest.

- Although she knows that she has been foolish, she is desperate for comfort and reassurance. See if you can imagine what the policeman and the interpreter look like so that you can connect more fully to her objective. The policeman cannot understand her, but the interpreter is a woman. To what extent does that make it easier for Lin Han to be so open about her feelings? Read the whole play to discover that the interpreter is in fact the ex-girlfriend of Jie Hui's business partner and the one who fired the shot!

Lin Han

66 I am Wang Lin Han. I am nineteen years old. I am here as a representative of the Panda Joy rug company. This is my passport. This is my visa.

I'm sorry. My English is very good but I'm upset. [...] I'm very upset and I can't think of the words. [...] I am our company's international representative. Because of my language skills. [...] I have been in communication with the representative of a distribution company. He finds contacts and investors to distribute the products of small-scale Chinese manufacturing companies into Europe. [...] Sometimes I wrote to this man in our language and sometimes we wrote in English, to practise. We had a very... happy correspondence, we made each other smile... at least... he put smileys in his messages too. So after a few months my father made a joke. He said this man would be the perfect husband for me because it would be so good for the family business. You see my father and my mother would like me to marry very soon but they know I think I shouldn't get married before I'm thirty. So they say things like that, as if they're joking, but I know they mean it too. [...] So I stopped the messages with the smileys in them. It was all business. And then he sent me another message with sad faces, and he asked if I was angry with him... [...] I thought, I've studied English for so long because I wanted to travel. And here I was just working in the same little factory I grew up in, in the same little town. I thought, this man could help me travel. It would be great for business so my mum and dad would be happy, I could escape without anyone crying about it.

And I've been in love and it was really horrible. It's really horrible to want someone and be in their power like that. [...] So... I thought I should think about a relationship with this man. It would be a practical choice. It would get me what I want. I asked him to send me a picture. [...] It was a beautiful picture. I loved his picture. [...] And it wasn't a studio picture! It wasn't lit and airbrushed and all shined up in Photoshop. It was just a casual picture. He was on the beach. He was smiling at me with such a look… […] I fell in love with his picture. I have to be honest now. I hoped he would love me first but that's what happened. I fell in love with a picture and a set of letters. Like a crazy girl who doesn't know what's real. […] He was right. He was right, I know nothing about him. And now I love him. Do you know the story about the baby ducks? […] The first thing a baby duck sees moving when it breaks through its shell it will love as its mother. You can make them love cats that want to eat them or chase after bicycle wheels and die in the road. I was just breaking out into the world. I'm a baby duck and I'm following a killer. […] I saw him with the body of this man. He said it had nothing to do with him, he was talking and talking and I looked in his eyes and I saw a lie.

Now I've realised I'm a stupid little duckling with shell in my baby feathers. I've stepped out into the world and it'll squash me. I thought I knew how to do anything but I'm just a stupid little girl. […] And I really do love him. Even though he probably is a killer and a liar. **99**

Picnic at Hanging Rock

Tom Wright
Adapted from Joan Lindsay's novel

TEN THINGS YOU NEED TO KNOW ABOUT AMBER (AND MICHAEL FITZHUBERT):

- Amber is a teenage girl who, along with four other young women, acts out the story of *Picnic at Hanging Rock*. In other words, it is the name of the actress, so in your version 'Amber' would be replaced with your own name.

- Amber is Australian.

- The year of the story is 1900, but Amber herself could be from any age after.

- She is dressed in an old-fashioned school uniform with a hat.

- The novel *Picnic at Hanging Rock* is about the disappearance of three schoolgirls and their governess while visiting the Mount Macedon area near Melbourne in Australia on Valentine's Day. Only one of them was ever seen again, and it remained a complete mystery as to what happened to the others. Although it is a work of fiction, it is told as if it were a true story. Read the whole play to understand more.

- In the monologue that follows, Amber is playing the part of Michael Fitzhubert, who was at Hanging Rock that same afternoon.

- Michael is a young Englishman.

- He has recently arrived in Australia where he is visiting his uncle and aunt.

- Michael is well-educated and considers himself a proper gentleman.

- It was Michael who, one week later, discovered Irma Leopold, one of the three missing girls, lying unconscious on the ground.

FIVE THINGS TO HELP YOU PERFORM THE MONOLOGUE:

- You will need to read the whole play, and may even like to read the novel from which it is adapted. There is also a film of *Picnic at Hanging Rock* which gives an excellent idea of the climate, territory, and potentially dangerous and rough terrain.

- Michael is romantic. He rather fancies himself as an adventurer and the one who can solve the mystery. In the monologue that follows, it is one week after the disappearance and Michael has decided to return on his own to Hanging Rock. See if you can capture this sense of swagger and adventure.

- Although Amber will have an Australian accent when she is playing the other parts, here she should have an RP English accent. Think about your physicality. How far do you want to go in your impersonation of a man? You may also like to try some of the other monologues in the play where the girls are acting out the female roles. There is plenty to choose from.

- The language is poetic and highly descriptive. Look at the way it is printed on the page like verse as opposed to prose. Consider also the punctuation, or rather the lack of it. In this sense the language is heightened, lyrical and rhythmic, and its imagery is rich and vivid. I would encourage you to be brave in your delivery, and to enjoy speaking the monologue as you would a poem.

- 'Menhirs' are large standing stones, 'basalt' is a kind of volcanic rock, 'antediluvian' refers to an ancient time before the Biblical flood, and 'Miranda' is one of the girls who went missing.

NB This play offers a number of other monologues from which to choose.

Amber

❝ I am a stranger here
A young Englishman
Educated
But knowing nothing.
Macedon, the mansion of my uncle.
I believe it is ninety-nine degrees
So hot
It is a garden party
The cream of Australia
They ape home like children playing dress-ups in the nursery
There is nothing to think about in this country.
The leaves on the trees are smeared teardrops
The food, the clothes, the letters on the page, all are familiar,
but –
I am utterly listless
Keep seeing a swan
Elegant, gracile
Golden locks
Caught in time poised over water.

[...]

I have a plan.
I will search the Rock
On my own, in my own way
Strange eyes
No police.
No bloodhounds

[...]

Hanging Rock
Temperature warm
Light wind from south-east
I have drawn up a plan, and laid a grid over the area
Formless menhirs on the north-east side
Life is welling up
Out of the warm green depth
Fronds of curled brown velvet
Snap under touch

I am clumsy here
Foreign insertion
My boots have crushed a nest
Of jackjumper ants
Impossible to know how many spiders
Massacred in their burrows
My hand brushes a streamer of bark
Writhing colony of caterpillars
Thick fur coats
With every step
I am cutting a swathe of death

Hanging Rock
Perhaps here
Miranda
Plunged into the dogwood
Prehistoric rocks
Erode their way
Through rotting vegetation
Animal decay
Bones
Feathers
Birdlime
Sloughed skins of snakes
Obscene knobs
Scabby carbuncles
Fetid holes
Did Miranda
Pillow her golden head
Here?
Mira–

I am alone on Hanging Rock
I can slit the basalt
As a hot knife in butter.
There are small jewels sparkling in ancient stone.
The wind blows among pipes that penetrate deep into the
dark belly of this earth
Darkness has been stored all day
Hanging Rock pressing

Against the empty sky
Empty of stars
I think I have moved
Strange, cannot tell which is up
And which is the bedrock.
The air moves though everything,
And time, it is either still
Or it is so turbulent that past, present, future,
They are all in disorder
And I am as much here with you now in your complacent
world
As I am in some antediluvian time
When this stone was all liquid
And stars were yet to be born –

[...]

Hanging –
All around me
Yes definitely heard it twice
Corner of my eye
Who is there?
I can hear you
I can almost see you
I know you're there
Who would be laughing here under the sea?
Who is that?
I am dreaming
Must find my way home
This is what it feels like to drown
I can feel you
I know you're there
Miranda
Miranda
Miranda
Mirand
Miran
Mira
Mir
Mi 〞

Plastic

Kenneth Emson

This play deals with adult themes. It has content and language that some readers might find disturbing or offensive.

TEN THINGS YOU NEED TO KNOW ABOUT LISA:

- Lisa is fifteen.

- She comes from a small town along the Thames Estuary in Essex.

- She is described as pretty and clever.

- She is good at school, and one day she hopes to go to college and then on to university.

- Lisa is a virgin.

- Lisa has fallen in love with a young man called Kev. Kev is nineteen, and even though she is under-age, he says he loves her too.

- Lisa wants to have sex with Kev.

- Lisa has two male friends that she has known all her life – Jack and Ben.

- Lisa gets on better with boys and thinks the girls at school are mostly 'bitches' or 'slags'.

- Lisa is different from the people she has grown up with in that she is ambitious and has high expectations for her life. The play offers two different outcomes for Lisa. Read it to find out what happens to her.

FIVE THINGS TO HELP YOU PERFORM THE MONOLOGUE:

- Lisa's accent is important. This is a play set firmly in Essex and what is known as an Estuary English accent is part of the music of the piece. I wouldn't suggest changing it. However, if you really love the speech and can't do the accent, make sure you choose something that fits in with her background.

- Although the language is contemporary, it is also heightened, poetic and rhythmic. This gives the play a muscularity, as if the language is a kind of heartbeat, pulsating and creating urgency and dramatic tension. Enjoy speaking it, searching out the rhythms and rhymes. Although it must be realistic, it is not the kind of monologue that should be mumbled or thrown away.

- Think about what Kev looks and sounds like. Although he is only nineteen, he is still an 'older man'. This fits in with the fact that Lisa is ambitious and wants more from her life than the girls around her. How does he make her feel? Perhaps you too have been attracted to an older boy and have been flattered by their response. What courage does it take to send the text? Or is it a safer way of giving Kev the 'green light' than saying it to his face? Either way it sets up the sexual tension for both characters.

- Lisa starts the monologue by talking to her friend Kerry. Later on in the play Lisa calls Kerry a 'slag', and even here the friendship is dubious. Perhaps you can relate to the idea of having a schoolfriend who isn't really a true friend. Someone who doesn't really understand you or lets you down in some way.

- Think about your physicality. When you are so attracted to someone you become physically restless. She uses words such as 'love hunch', 'flutter', and 'beat-skipping'. Perhaps you know that feeling or have observed it in someone else. It is important that you connect to her mounting state of excitement when performing the monologue.

Lisa

" Ring Kerry
Before I text him
To tell him
That I'll let him
Tonight.
She's laughing
Lol.
Saying
'Why tonight?'
'What's the occasion?'
That maybe I love him
I say
'Like we love them all'
She says back
With a wisecrack
She must think is some kind of wisdom.
Coming from the girl who's more akin
To a leg up round the alleyway
On lunch
Than this love hunch that my heart's producing
With its flutters
And its beat-skipping.
So I just say
Jealous?
And she says
'Yeah'
And I say
Today's the day
Why not?
Why wait?
Today's the day.

And she says
'I tell the other girls then yeah?'
And I say
Don't…
And she says

'Why not?'
And I say
Because this is special
And she says
'You're special'
And I…

[…]

And the line goes dead.
Cut off.
Indefinitely.
And the dialling tone seems to be laughing a little bit
And I think about the consequences
And all that other shit
That people say to think about.
Not that it matters
Not now…

Text
Sent.

[…]

Get to school ten minutes before the bell
Chain-smoked six fags on the way.
Marlboro Light head rush
Adds to the bad feeling my stomach's spitting up.
Push it back down.
Think of…
Excited flutters
His warm hot breath
And the mutters
Of love
Or some other such.
As his hands undress me
And this once
I will let them
Rest
Where they want to rest
Without complaint
Or stress

[…]

Morning lessons pass quietly
Thinking about things…
I shouldn't be thinking 'bout.
In classrooms with teachers not much older
Than the girls who meet down the crèche
With equal disappointment
Of this life
This mess

[…]

The fact that it's actually going to happen

[…]

Three thirty

[…]

Even though I'm scared

[…]

The moment
I give it away
To him
Today.
Today I'm his
His and no one else's.

And the boys that I might of once kissed
While pissed
Up the park.
Ain't nothing to me

[…]

Today is the day

[…]

No more V plates

[…]

No more innocence

[...]

No
Not after today.

[...]

His mum's out till ten tonight

[...]

Plenty of time

[...]

No need to freak out

[...]

Everyone does this

[...]

Everyone does this.
Everyone.

Calm
Down.

Then colours outside the schoolroom seem brighter
Breath lighter.
Today's the day
My day. 🙰

Pronoun

Evan Placey

TEN THINGS YOU NEED TO KNOW ABOUT DEAN:

- Dean is seventeen.

- Dean is a transgender male (female-to-male), played by a female actor.

- Dean lives with his mum, dad and younger sister Dani. Dean's parents are trying hard to accept that their daughter is now their son. Dani, however, is finding it hard and misses her older sister.

- Dean strongly identifies with the American actor James Dean, and has a poster of him in his bedroom. When he is feeling stressed or lonely he imagines he is talking to the real actor who died aged twenty-four in a car accident.

- Dean has been injecting himself with testosterone as part of his transitioning process. It has been playing havoc with his hormones and he is often moody.

- He wants to have an operation to complete the process but it costs a lot. For now he has to make do with short hair, appearing like a boy by binding his breasts, and putting a sock in his pants.

- He uses the boys' toilets at school and pees through a tube which means he can stand up.

- When he was a girl he had a boyfriend called Josh. Josh still wants to go out with Dean, but Dean is confused.

- Dean is highly intelligent, sensitive and funny. He is also honest and brave.

- He has been arguing with Josh, and at this point in the play Dean has a black eye from where Josh punched him. Read the whole play to understand more about Josh and Dean's relationship.

FIVE THINGS TO HELP YOU PERFORM THE MONOLOGUE:

- Dean has been asked by the school to make this speech as part of an assembly for an Ofsted visit. The Senior Management Team want to use Dean to show just how good the school is at diversity, inclusivity and tolerance. However, Dean is a rebel and refuses to be the happy face of liberal values. See how he uses the opportunity to challenge the school, demanding respect for himself as an individual.

- Think about how you will use the words 'tolerance' and 'tolerate'. Where are you being matter-of-fact, where ironic? See if you can find the variety of ways those words are interpreted and the particular tone of voice that best describes his attitude to them.

- The 'black woman' on the bus, the 'woman who chained herself to Parliament' and 'the angry drag queens in a bar' refer respectively to Rosa Parks, a suffragette, and New York's gay community who drank at the Stonewall Inn. Take time to research more about these activists.

- Dean is brave. It takes courage to speak out in this way. See if you can connect to that feeling of contempt that he has.

- See if you can imagine performing the speech as if you are in a big school hall addressing several hundred people. Although Dean must be nervous, he is also fired up. The speech feels political and needs power in its delivery.

Dean

❝ Good afternoon, students, teachers, and visitors from Ofsted.

Our school prides itself on tolerance. You can be who you want to be and we will tolerate you. It says so in a policy document in a drawer somewhere.

We learn in history about a black woman who decided one day to sit where she wanted to on a bus.

We learn about another woman who chained herself to Parliament.

We learn about some angry drag queens in a bar who fought back one night.

We learn that to be tolerant of every person is what we should aspire to. A badge of honour we can wear. *I am a tolerant person.*

Fuck tolerance.

Those people – the black lady on the bus, the woman in chains, those men in heels. They weren't fighting for tolerance. To be tolerated.

Because tolerance is horseshit.

Tolerance is the emptiest word in the dictionary.

Tolerate is what you do when someone's playing their music loudly on the bus.

Tolerate is what you do when someone's texting next to you in the cinema.

I don't want to be tolerated.

I want to be admired.

I want to be envied.

I want to be… loved.

Love me.

And if that's too much to ask. Then hate me.

But don't tolerate me.

Because tolerance means sweet fuck-all. **99**

Ramona Tells Jim

Sophie Wu

TEN THINGS YOU NEED TO KNOW ABOUT POCAHONTAS:

- Pocahontas is nineteen years old.

- She wears a lot of make-up and is described as 'aggressive'.

- She comes from Mallaig, which is a town on the west coast of Scotland.

- She comes from a disadvantaged background.

- She still lives with her mum, whom she says she hates, and her brother, but she can't wait to move out.

- She is desperate to better herself and dreams of having a good job and living in a nice house.

- At the moment she is working in a supermarket. She'd like to work in a bank, but doesn't have the necessary qualifications.

- She has been seeing an older man called Jim.

- Pocahontas is pregnant, although she cannot be one-hundred-per-cent sure that Jim is the father.

- Pocahontas is relying on Jim to take her away from her unhappy life at home, but Jim doesn't love her. It could be said that they are both using the other for their own personal gain.

FIVE THINGS TO HELP YOU PERFORM THE MONOLOGUE:

- Her accent is important. If you aren't Scottish or good at a Scots accent, you could try performing the monologue in a different dialect. The key thing is that her tone is rough, and she speaks with a strong accent.

- The monologue is made up from a conversation that she is having with Jim. Imagine what he looks like and how he is responding. You should, of course, read the whole scene so that you can get a firm idea of what is being said to you. As long as you are hearing Jim's voice in your head, the monologue will work on its own.

- Although Pocahontas is described as 'aggressive', she is very funny (mostly unintentionally), and the speech should be comic. Have fun with it.

- Be careful, however, that you do not judge her or turn her into a stereotype. She is vulnerable and has good reason to behave in the way that she does. As a character there is something hugely likable about her.

- What might it feel like to be pregnant even at this early stage? See if you can capture her excitement at the prospect of something growing inside her.

Pocahontas

❝ Jim! Oh my god, Jim, there you are! Why are you not picking up? I've called you seventeen times and you haven't replied to a single one of my twenty-six texts! [...] You've got absolutely brilliant signal and you've been standing here for over a quarter of an hour. [...] I've been monitoring your movements all morning. Have you heard of the app 'Find Your Friends'? It's absolutely fantastic. I installed it on your phone yesterday so I can keep track of your whereabouts at all times. [...] I was getting worried. I thought you might have committed suicide because of your depressed state. [...] I am now linked to you for ever by the strongest possible bond and will need constant and instant responses twenty-four hours a day, seven days a week. [...] I am with child. I am prrrregnant. [...] Four tests, Jim. Four little windows saying pregnant pregnant pregnant, pregnant.

[...]

Is it mine? Did you just say that? [...] Is it mine? [...] I can't believe you're asking me that. I'm fucking shocked.

[...]

Is it mine?! You've just asked it again!

[…]

Is it mine?!

[…]

Of course it's yours, you fat fucking prick.

Beat.

Probably. (*Off Jim's look.*) I mean obviously I can't be a hundred per cent.

[…]

Men are drawn to me. Moths and flames, Jimmy. Moths and flames…

[…]

Honestly, you don't know how lucky you are to have me as the future mother of your child. I'm nineteen, I'm fucking fit, I've got a pierced clitoris and I'm double-jointed. You can basically bend me up like a pretzel and take me up the yin-yang. What's not to love? You're an ex-con who works in a fish factory – […] And you're *thirty-two*. You're basically dead. […] It's amazing, Jim, isn't it? Just to think: there's a little piece of you. Growing inside of me. Like one of your crusty wee sea monsters – […] Except rather than being a dead thing from the past trapped inside a jar, this one will actually slither out and live. I hope she's a girl, Jim. I'd love to have a wee girl. Dress her up in satin party dresses and buy her jam tarts and brush her hair. What you think of the name Jasmina? Or Rapunzel! I'm never, ever going to cut her hair, it's just going to trail along behind her like a long, golden waterfall. Can you imagine? […]

A couple of beats of silence.

Don't be sad, Jim. Why are you always so sad when everything is so amazing? ”

Ramona Tells Jim

Sophie Wu

TEN THINGS YOU NEED TO KNOW ABOUT RAMONA:

- Ramona is sixteen years old, and the year is 1998.

- She is English. (Although out of context she could come from anywhere.)

- She comes from a middle-class background.

- She lives with her mother, who is a single parent.

- Ramona says that her mother is lonely and depressed. She says she hates her mother.

- She goes to an all-girls school called St Hilda's, and is well-educated.

- Ramona struggles to fit in with the other girls at her school and says she prefers the company of boys.

- Ramona is a virgin.

- She likes listening to the music of Enya.

- Ramona is eccentric, very bright, energetic, and has a quick and quirky sense of humour.

FIVE THINGS TO HELP YOU PERFORM THE MONOLOGUE:

- On a geography field trip to Scotland, Ramona has met local boy Jim. They are instantly attracted to one another. Jim has told her about the myth of the selkie, a seal-like creature who can shed its skin to become human on land. In her dream she imagines that Jim is a selkie. See if you can picture what Jim looks like and the power of those green eyes. Perhaps you have had a similar attraction to someone and even dreamt about them.

- The speech has many different qualities. It is descriptive, dramatic, poetic, sexy and also very funny. You will need to capture all these different atmospheres for the speech to come alive. You might also take inspiration from listening to Enya's *Watermark* album.

- Ramona is highly imaginative and likes to play with words. She makes a joke of almost everything. Even things that hurt or upset her become the subjects of her wit and fun. It is like a kind of nervous tic with her, and she doesn't think before she speaks. Read the whole play to understand her particular brand of humour.

- Think about the dream itself and how some dream states have that way of making you think that what is happening is happening for real. She describes it as a 'lucid dream', being in between asleep and awake. In any event it could also be seen as a sexual fantasy. Have you ever fantasised about someone or something, even if you know the fantasy is an impossibility?

- The monologue ends ominously. It is threatening and at odds with the fun she is experiencing at the beginning. In the context of the whole play it is portentous. See if you can build to that dramatic ending from the point where she reaches out to him through to the final – 'Everything is black.'

Ramona

❝ I am not asleep. Nor am I really awake. I am in that pleasant state in between, immersed in a semi-erotic lucid dream. I am standing on the shores of a small shingle bay. A giant silver orb, otherwise known as the moon, is casting a mystical glow upon this mellow scene. I gaze out at the waveless water for some time, the air is still and it is utterly silent, then very slowly the surface of the sea begins to ripple. A head emerges from it – a boy with piercing green eyes. He stares right through me and it sends a tingling sensation into the very depths of my loins. He is swimming towards me and, as he does so, I look down and discover that I am possessed of a pair of simply enormous breasts which are being restrained only by a clam-shell bikini. The boy reaches the fringes of the beach and, as he rises from the water, hauling himself onto the shingle with two muscular arms, I emit a stifled gasp – (*Gasps.*) for instead of legs he has the oily black tail of a seal. His torso, however – is *all man.* He is a selkie. (*Echo.*) 'Hello, boy.' My voice is rich and caramel and echoes poetically.

'Hello, girl.'

His voice also echoes – although not quite so rich and caramel. Using my semi-conscious mind I will him to shed his tail. The tail drops to the floor into a shiny, black puddle, and to my delight he is clad only in a pair of tiny Calvin Klein briefs. He walks towards me – sinewy and pale and powerful – and I reach out to fondle his prominent pectorals. But as my fingers hover towards him, I am all of a sudden violently sucked into the shingle. Spiralling down and down. As I spiral, I reach out, and snatch his seal skin before I am enveloped. I scream. A horrible scream that reverberates through the entire universe. Everything is black. **99**

Ruined

Lynn Nottage

This play deals with adult themes. It has content and language that some readers might find disturbing or offensive.

TEN THINGS YOU NEED TO KNOW ABOUT SALIMA:

- Salima is nineteen.

- She is Congolese, from the Democratic Republic of Congo, in Africa.

- She is described as 'a sturdy peasant woman whose face betrays a world-weariness'.

- A brutal civil war rages in the Congo. One day in her village, while her husband was away, Salima was ambushed by soldiers who murdered her baby girl and kept Salima prisoner. For five months she was tied like an animal and repeatedly raped. When Salima was finally freed, her husband and family disowned her, forcing her from her own village.

- Salima has been sold to Mama Nadi, a brothel owner. In order to survive Salima has to work as a prostitute, 'entertaining' soldiers.

- Salima is pregnant by one of the soldiers who raped her.

- Despite her desperate circumstances she is brave and hopeful.

- She and another girl called Sophie (who is also a victim of rape as a weapon of war) are plotting their escape from the brothel.

- Salima's husband, Fortune, has made his way to the camp where she is working as a prostitute, but Salima is refusing to see him. Sophie can't understand and is trying to persuade Salima that maybe he has forgiven her. However, Salima believes that even if he is sorry for abandoning her, when he finds out that she is pregnant by one of the soldiers who raped her, he will reject her all over again.

- It will help to read director Kate Whoriskey's introduction in the playscript. It is a fascinating and moving account of how she and writer Lynn Nottage travelled to Central Africa and how the play came about through conversations with the people they met there.

FIVE THINGS TO HELP YOU PERFORM THE MONOLOGUE:

- Salima is talking to Sophie. It is a very private conversation and she can trust her. Think about the fact that for one whole month she has kept this 'story' to herself. How easy/difficult must it be to recount these terrible things. Might it feel shameful or is it a relief to have someone to tell? You will need to visualise what Sophie looks like so that when you are speaking you can imagine her reactions. Read the whole play to understand more about their friendship. Without upsetting yourself, you will need to be able to picture what has happened to Salima.

- Consider the language. The monologue is beautifully written. Its poetry is in sharp contrast to the violence it describes.

- Think about Salima's physicality. She is a survivor, but is constantly reminded of the pain in her vagina, and – now that she is pregnant – her womb. What must it feel like to be growing the child of the man who raped you?

- It is easy to focus on the violation to Salima – the monologue is largely about it – but this risks forgetting the death of her baby Beatrice. Make sure that you give sufficient weight to this moment. It is given only a few sentences, but consider that this is because it is an even worse atrocity, and one which is just too terrible for Salima to dwell on.

- As obvious as it sounds, the monologue requires you to have a Congolese or, at the very least, a general African accent. 'Sorghum' is a grain grown in Africa for food. It is a beautiful red colour. Get a sense of the Congolese landscape, its colours, the frangipani tree and the peacock. Again, all this beauty is in sharp contrast to the horrors depicted.

Salima

❝ Do you know what I was doing on that morning? (*A calm washes over her.*) I was working in our garden, picking the last of the sweet tomatoes. I put Beatrice down in the shade of a frangipani tree, because my back was giving me some trouble. Forgiven? Where was Fortune? He was in town fetching a new iron pot. 'Go,' I said. 'Go, today, man, or you won't have dinner tonight!' I had been after him for a new pot for a month. And finally on that day the damn man had to go and get it. A new pot. The sun was about to crest, but I had to put in another hour before it got too hot. It was such a clear and open sky. This splendid bird, a peacock, had come into the garden to taunt me, and was showing off its feathers. I stooped down and called to the bird: 'Wssht, Wssht.' And I felt a shadow cut across my back, and when I stood four men were there over me, smiling, wicked schoolboy smiles. 'Yes?' I said. And the tall soldier slammed the butt of his gun into my cheek. Just like that. It was so quick, I didn't even know I'd fallen to the ground. Where did they come from? How could I not have heard them?

[…]

One of the soldiers held me down with his foot. He was so heavy, thick like an ox and his boot was cracked and weathered like it had been left out in the rain for weeks. His boot was pressing my chest and the cracks in the leather had the look of drying sorghum. His foot was so heavy, and it was all I could see as the others… 'took' me. My baby was crying. She was a good baby. Beatrice never cried, but she was crying, screaming. 'Shhh,' I said. 'Shhh.' And right then… (*Closes her eyes.*) A soldier stomped on her head with his boot. And she was quiet.

A moment. SALIMA *releases:*

Where was everybody? WHERE WAS EVERYBODY?! […] I fought them! […] I did! […] But they still took me from my home. They took me through the bush—raiding thieves. Fucking demons! 'She is for everyone, soup to be had before dinner,' that is what someone said. They tied me to a tree by my foot, and the men came whenever they wanted soup. I make fires, I cook food, I listen to their stupid songs, I carry bullets, I clean wounds, I wash blood from their clothing, and, and, and… I lay there as they tore me to pieces, until I was raw… five months. Five months. Chained like a goat. These men fighting… fighting for our liberation. Still I close my eyes and I see such terrible things. Things I cannot stand to have in my head. How can men be this way?

A moment.

It was such a clear and open sky. So, so beautiful. How could I not hear them coming? 🭬🭬

Russian Dolls

Kate Lock

TEN THINGS YOU NEED TO KNOW ABOUT CAMELIA:

- Camelia is seventeen.
- She comes from a broken home.
- She grew up on a council estate in London, and has spent time in a children's care home.
- She has a vibrant energy, and although she appears tough, she is scared and vulnerable.
- Her mother is a drug addict and prostitute. She shows no interest in Camelia, and because she has a violent boyfriend called Troy, Camelia was taken into care.
- When she was in the care home, Camelia violently attacked a girl who insulted her mother. The girl called Camelia's mother a 'junky whore', so Camelia hit her with a boiling hot kettle. This led to a prison sentence in a young offenders' institution.
- When she was in the institution she felt safe and was given lots of attention from her care workers, but Camelia's life on the 'outside' is lonely and frightening.
- Although Camelia is close to Zach, one of her brothers, he is a gang member and can't be trusted. Later on in the play he uses Camelia to steal for the gang and pimps her off to them.
- This monologue comes at the very start of the play as Camelia is being released.
- Read the whole play to find out what happens when she meets a blind woman called Hilda. You will also find some other good monologues that you might like.

FIVE THINGS TO HELP YOU PERFORM THE MONOLOGUE:

- Even though Camelia's mother has neglected her, Camelia still loves her. She is desperate for her mother's love and a big part of her still hopes that she will get it. Have a picture in your head of what Camelia's mother looks like. Camelia has a strong imagination. See if you can picture the fantasy of her mother arriving to collect her.

- You will also need to imagine what both the Caribbean warden and Alice the social worker look and sound like.

- Troy is a violent drug addict. Consider how it makes Camelia feel when she mentions him, and the fact that her little brother and sister have been taken into care because her mother is back with him.

- Having served a sentence, how will it feel to know that you can't go home, and that you have to go into a strange hostel?

- See if you can chart the journey from hope to disappointment as Camelia realises that her fantasy has faded into nothing.

NB This play offers a number of other monologues from which to choose.

Camelia

❝ A bin liner. Fuckin bin liner! Dat's what dey give me for my stuff. Warden goes to me, 'You never come inside, wiv no bag of your own.' I go, 'Course I did, someone must of nicked it.' That proper slows things down which is not what I want yeah, cos Mum might be waitin outside the gate. And she never waits for no one. They wait for her. That's how it goes wiv Mum. Wiv men… Then the warden, she arks me to sign all da stuff is mine. Like I can remember? I wanna get out but I ain't goin nowhere wiv no bin liner. That ain't never a good look. So this Caribbean warden, she's on da gate, she goes, 'Take you this one, gal.' It was not my kinda bag, let me tell ya. No way my style. More like some straw basket wiv pictures of fruit an shit on da front but she is lookin straight at me. 'Start up ya new life, new style.' So I go, 'You want me bring it back yeah?' 'Lissen. I don't wanta never see it again. Or you. You get me?' Then she gives me this proper serious stare. So I nod ma head and I'm outta there... into the light! Mum wasn't pickin up and she weren't nowhere to be seen outside da gates. She ain't got no car!... but that's how it come up, in my head, in colour, wiv music yeah. Mum, drivin up in some stylish BMW wiv da roof off yeah and Beyoncé like blarin out... And she brakes sudden like and leans over to open da door wiv a tray a doughnuts on da back and her in some new bikini cos we ain't goin home, nah, we drivin to da coast, meet her new friends wiv wine coolers an beach houses, an an... But I'm still standin here wiv my fruit bag, don't know for how long. Then I see Alice, my key social. Her like wavin across the traffic tryin get my attention. [...] So Alice goes to me she's bringin me straight from the Young Offenders to some new hostel. Not home. Not allow. There've been developments. Hate that word. It's not houses like you'd think. New homes on some estate not quite finished. Fuckin developments... Mum's only gone an let Troy come back so they've had to remove the little 'uns and keep me away. Alice goes, 'It would be inadvisable to visit your mum' but I don't spar wiv her. I mean... What a fuckin job! No one likes a social, I mean no one. What I can't believe is they went university an got some degree to get a shit job like that. And her nails! When there's no nail left, she like bites the skin on the outside. Eats it. She don't touch the biscuits. She's the one who's mental. **99**

Scorch

Stacey Gregg

TEN THINGS YOU NEED TO KNOW ABOUT KES:

- Kes was born a girl, but identifies as a boy.

- Kes is seventeen.

- In the play, Kes comes from Belfast in Northern Ireland, but the playwright suggests changing this to fit in with wherever you are from.

- Although Kes is unsure yet about whether he wants to transition, he dresses like a boy, binding his chest and hiding his hair under a hat. Kes has also bought an artificial penis online which he wears in his pants.

- All this means that Kes has to go to some lengths to keep up the 'pretence' – changing in toilets when he leaves and returns home.

- Kes has had a sexual relationship with a girl called Jules. Kes made love to Jules using an artificial penis intended for penetration.

- Despite having said that she was in love with him, when Jules finds out that Kes is not a boy, she dumps him.

- Although Kes is hurt at having been dumped, the fact of having had a girlfriend and even experiencing some heartache has made Kes feel 'normal'.

- The support group that Kes attends has given him a sense of freedom. For the first time in his life he feels that no one is judging him and that he can be himself.

- Read the whole play to learn much more about what it means to be transgender, the importance of regarding people in a non-binary way and the recent cases of 'gender fraud'. There is an excellent introduction in the playtext written by experts on the subject.

FIVE THINGS TO HELP YOU PERFORM THE MONOLOGUE:

- Despite having been dumped, Kes is still 'loved up'. It is important that he believes he still has a chance with Jules, and that, perhaps, if he transitions, Jules will take him back.

- Think about the support group. Although you are speaking to the audience, in your mind's eye you are there. What does the room look like? See if you can imagine the other members of the group. We have a description of Max, but you will need to read the whole play to find out who else is there.

- The humour. Although the subject matter is serious there is a lot of comedy in the play, and Kes himself has a quirky sense of humour. For example, the way he turns the term lesbian/gay/bisexual/transgender/queer into LGBTQ adding ABCDEFG to the abbreviation – like ordering a coffee, things can get very complicated!

- The importance of the pronoun – she/he/they. To a person who doesn't feel wholly male or female, this is vital. The fluidity around these terms blows Kes's mind.

- If you don't already know the feeling of being trapped in the wrong identity, you will have to think about how Kes's physicality differs from your own. What does it feel like to be Kes? How does he walk, sit, stand and what does he feel like emotionally? Read the whole play to understand more. You may also like to watch films such as Boys Don't Cry with the actress Hilary Swank. This particular film gives a very good account of what it feels like to be female identifying as male. However, be warned that there are some upsetting scenes and the film is rated 18.

NB This play offers a number of other monologues from which to choose.

Kes

❝ Come to the meet-up group a second time. Read about T. Testosterone. But don't know. I'm just curious. Maybe cos I feel more, more – confident. Know how perfect it can feel.

If I transition maybe I can rock up on Jules' doorstep and offer her everything I can't offer her now. I can be her boyfriend. And we could be together. AND GET A CAT.

But but but it's another level and, it kinda I dunno it kinda s–s–scares me.

(*Back in the group.*)

The group properly sits up. This is what they love. Who gives a toot about lezzers? Boooooring. This is way better. And I'm ready to talk now. I've come to this group. Crapping myself but I found this group, LGBTQABCDEFG and this is a group where we start by letting the group know if we are she, he, they

BLOWS MY MIND.

'They. Prefer not to define.'

(KES*'s head implodes.*) Click.

Universe falls into place. He, she, they. And loads of words I don't even understand –

I can never concentrate in school but I'm learning *loads* here –

And we nod and use the right pronoun and I, I exist in the circle. Breathe, sit up in your seat, crack jokes, look people in the eyeballs.

And you shouldn't say tranny actually. Cos it's hurtful.

You can buy T online.

(KES *is coherent and technicolour, electric with discovery.*)

Max, this skinny dude in the circle next to a boy in completely gay loafers has been on hormones for months and you can totally see. He. Looks. Awesome. I'd never want to be one of those stacked dudes, but Max just looks *solid*. Great shoulders, and I don't know if he binds or what, but he looks like he's already had top surgery.

Can't stop looking at his body. His jaw.

T makes your boobs shrink. Your face more angular. Your voice drops. You lose fat off your hips and get more muscley. First thing I'd do is buzz off my hair. Short back and sides. Slick into a smart side parting. Sharp. Phwoar!

But shut up, shut up brain, getting carried away. Don't really know if I would. Just tucked my hair into a hat with Jules. Miss Jules. Would I miss my hair?

Like it long sometimes.

Don't tell anyone. Don't tell anyone that before I go home, I stop in a public toilet. Stuff my hat in my bag. Change. Don't feel trapped, just...

not there yet. Or something. Growing into it. Carry it around like it'll explode over some unsuspecting teacher when I'm in Normal Life Mode – buying shoes / eating McCoys / at Asda. Hide – go home someone else. Fraud. Some strange chick who wears a bridesmaid dress to her cousin's wedding.

I'm trying to find the opposite of lying. Um. The truth, I suppose. I know I don't say it right but don't know how... don't know how I can do it right yet.

The circle listen to Lara, a really pretty, hilarious transwoman. Lara's talking about disclosure and stealth and stuff. I feel lucky. Lara's saying she finally loves herself, and now she's ready to be loved. Now she's ready to allow herself to be loved. Damn right. Cos she's gorgeous and everything.

I have an ex.

I've loved.

I'm normal. **99**

Scuttlers

Rona Munro

TEN THINGS YOU NEED TO KNOW ABOUT THERESA:

- Theresa is a teenage slum-dweller. She lives in a cramped lodging house in Ancoats, Manchester.

- The year is 1882.

- She describes herself as 'fat and beautiful', although out of context it does not matter what she looks like.

- Theresa belongs to a gang called The Tigers from Bengal Street. She is a 'scuttler', which was the name given to gang members who ruled the streets in Manchester in the late-nineteenth century.

- Theresa is a fierce fighter and is not afraid of getting blood on her hands. Other gang members look up to her.

- The gang's greatest enemy is the Prussia Street mob, with whom they have called for a fight.

- Despite being a fighter, Theresa is also fiercely kind and intensely loyal to the people she chooses to protect. She says she prefers friends to family, because you get to choose your friends.

- When she's not fighting, Theresa works in a mill. Working conditions are poor and it is a hard life.

- At this point in the play, the Burnley spinners are on strike and there is no thread, leaving the looms empty and factory workers like Theresa temporarily out of work.

- It is a hot summer, the factories are closed, but the pubs have been open. Fuelled by drink and restless from unemployment, Theresa and the others are ready for a fight.

FIVE THINGS TO HELP YOU PERFORM THE MONOLOGUE:

- Theresa is talking to Thomas, also a teenage slum-dweller. She has taken pity on him and has let him share her bed.

- They are talking about their mothers, playing a kind of a game to see whose mother was the most stupid. However, as the monologue goes on Theresa becomes increasingly emotional as she remembers her mother's illness. See if you can chart her journey from being quite dismissive of her mother to feeling a deep sadness at her loss.

- Theresa and Thomas are drinking. Without playing drunk, you might like to reference the fact by playing the monologue while taking occasional sips from a bottle. (Try it out, but ditch it if you feel it is becoming a distraction.)

- Despite her outward show of bravado, Theresa is hungry for love and for intimacy. See if you can strike the balance between being hard on the outside, but soft on the inside.

- Theresa wants Thomas to desire her, but also to respect her. She is both flirtatious and competitive. See if you can imagine what Thomas looks like. Perhaps you have or have had a similar relationship.

Theresa

66 Right, this is how stupid my mother was. You've no idea. She were that stupid. Know what she did? […] She left me and my big brother with four. Four! Like a basket of kittens. Four! 'Just feed them,' she says, 'You know how to do that.' Then she's off! […] And they were stupider than her. Easy to know they're hers. A kitten has the sense to come running when you've food for it, but did they? No. Did they have the sense not to fall in ditches or under a cart? No. […] My brother was fourteen… What did she think would happen? 'Just keep hold of them all,' she says. How was I supposed to do that? They were all running about already. […] (And then) she died. […] I don't know (what of). She were just sick.

I tried to look after her. We'd no money for a doctor with her too sick to work. She pulled me to her and her hands were that hot and her breath smelled like a drain but I loved her. I did.

Her face was that thin at the end but I thought she was beautiful because I knew it was the last I'd see of her. I was holding on to her hot hands, tight, tight because I knew she was going, I was begging her not to up and die and leave me but I knew she couldn't help it really. She weren't stupid then. She was sick. But that was the last thing she said to me, 'Just hold on to your sisters.' Now that were stupid because how could I do that? She died saying a stupid thing like that and it tore me to scraps. **99**

Space Wang*

Tom Wells

TEN THINGS YOU NEED TO KNOW ABOUT NORA:

- Nora is around fourteen.

- She is from Withernsea, which is a small coastal town in east Yorkshire.

- She lives with her father, who is a single parent.

- A year ago to the day, her mother committed suicide by walking into the sea and drowning.

- Nora is lost without her mother. She gets little comfort from her father, who is depressed, and she has taken to shoplifting and drinking vodka as a way of numbing the pain.

- Nora refuses to believe that her mother is dead or that she drowned herself. Instead she believes that her mother journeyed into space and that she will return tonight on the anniversary of her 'mysterious' disappearance.

- Nora says that she can both receive and interpret alien signals.

- Nora loves the song 'Don't Stop Believin'' by Journey.

- Nora has stopped going to school, but she says she likes dance and wouldn't mind doing a dance GCSE.

- Nora is funny, sensitive, loyal and trusting.

FIVE THINGS TO HELP YOU PERFORM THE MONOLOGUE:

- Nora is expecting her mother to return from outer space tonight, and she has divided the day into three phases in preparation to meet her. The monologue that follows is part of phase one. This gives the speech a certain dynamic. It is part of a larger framework and you may like to choose other sections to work on and to perform. Read the whole play to

* Published in the volume *The Kitchen Sink* by Tom Wells

understand Nora's state of mind. You will need to grasp that she is in denial about her mother's suicide and that this colours her whole out look. It is easier for her to imagine that her mother was abducted by aliens than it is for her to accept that she took her own life. Although you might not have had such an extreme experience, perhaps you can connect to that feeling of wanting to believe something so much that you actually convince yourself it is true.

- The monologue does an interesting thing with the past and present tense. First of all there is the shoplifting 'lesson' and an explanation about her relationship with Carl, then we suddenly flip to 'today' and Nora describes events as if they were happening now. It is a particular kind of storytelling, and you will need the right kind of energy to re-enact this blow-by-blow account. See if you can really picture all that she describes from the people, to the vodka bottle, the peanut butter and the trollies, etc. The more detail you can supply, the more effective the monologue will be.

- Nora appears in this part of the play like a natural rebel. She is bold and fearless of authority. However, you might like to consider that this rebellious streak is a response to the grief that she is experiencing rather than an inherent characteristic. The death of her mother and her inability to share her grief with her father have resulted in this 'bad girl' behaviour.

- If an east Yorkshire accent is not native to you, you might like to try the speech in a different accent. However, think about the rhythm of the monologue and the language Nora uses. I would suggest that it would suit any regional accent, but is not suitable for a standard English (middle-class) accent or a multicultural-London-English accent, which has its variants in Birmingham and Manchester. Remember that Nora is from a small town and that her accent must reflect this. It is part of her charm.

- Although not referenced in this part of the play, Nora is carrying around a rucksack containing the sandals that her mother left on the beach, a colander, a shoebox with some flashing fairy lights, and home-made dials and some sparklers.

It is with this paraphernalia that she means to attract her mother's attention. In order to create some inner life for yourself, you might like to have a rucksack with these objects inside. In this way you will feel closer to Nora and to the sense of urgency she is experiencing on this day in particular.

NB This play offers a number of other monologues from which to choose.

Nora

66 Shoplifting is a piece of piss. You just, you basically just: nick it. And then you get caught. And the security man goes: 'What you doing?' and you just have to say really loud: 'NO, CARL' or whatever his badge says. And if there's any old ladies nearby, or nuns and that, and there always is, they look over and Carl gets well confused. Starts steering you by your shoulders to his little office. And you hang on till you're just in the doorway then shout: 'COS I DON'T WANT TO SHOW YOU MY FANNY. AGAIN.' He panics and you just run off. Next time you nick something though he remembers what happened and you can see him thinking 'not worth it', just lets you get away with it. So you can get quite a lot of vodka really, it's no trouble. And actually I'm quite good mates with Carl now. He gives me this little nod near exotic fruit then in about five minutes he's out the back on his break. We get pissed between the wheelie bins.

And I did show him my fanny in the end but. Just to say thanks but. He wasn't fussed.

Today's a bit different though. Soon as I come in he's looking dead panicky, starts doing this, tries to sort of waft me back out the door. I just ignore it, plod on but he's in a right flap. And all this wafting? And I can see him looking at this woman. She's standing next to him with a clipboard and a little moustache, making all these notes so he doesn't know what to... Mouths something at me like: 'Go away' but, I dunno, I just mouth something back like: 'no', head for the booze. I'm umming and aahing a bit but there's signals coming off the Smirnoff so I know it's the right one. And it's buy-one-get-one-free so. Just ignore the bit about buying one. Check over my shoulder, tuck it in my pants. Quite a cold thing to tuck in your pants but. Never mind.

I can see Carl out the corner of my eye. He's getting really interested in this peanut butter. Like properly interested. Like he's getting a bit weird about the peanut butter, and the woman's thinking he's got some sort of thing about peanut butter, maybe he goes home, covers himself in peanut butter and gets local cats to lick it off. He doesn't though. Just buying me time.

And I know it's probably the last time I can do this now cos of moustache-woman and the clipboard and the peanut butter and everything. So what I do, I just, I flipping: leg it. Out the door, trollies flying, knocking over all the old ladies and the nuns and that just, flipping just: get out. On my way. And the alarm's beeping and Carl's shouting, sort of very slowly thundering after me but I'm just, I don't give a, cos, you know, today's too important. Today's too important and you need it to be just right.

You need it to be just right. **99**

Things I Know To Be True

Andrew Bovell

TEN THINGS YOU NEED TO KNOW ABOUT ROSIE:

- Rosie is nineteen.

- She is on a gap year.

- She comes from a working-class suburb of Adelaide in South Australia.

- She lives with her mum and dad.

- Rosie has an older sister and two older brothers, making her the baby of the family.

- Rosie is adored by her family and she in turn is very attached to them. Sometimes she worries that she loves them too much.

- She wants to leave home and become independent, but she is caught somewhere between child and adulthood and is finding it hard to grow up.

- She doesn't know what she wants to do with her life, although we find out later on in the play that she loves creative writing.

- Rosie is kind, intelligent and sensitive. She is also trusting – perhaps a little too trusting.

- Because she is the youngest, she is often in the middle of any family quarrel. This has given her the qualities of a peacemaker, and as we will see in the monologue that follows her behaviour tends to be more reactive than active.

FIVE THINGS TO HELP YOU PERFORM THE MONOLOGUE:

- The monologue acts as a kind of introduction to the play. It happens in Berlin before the main story starts and is the only scene that is set outside the family home. It is Rosie's way of telling us about what has happened to her, and it is important that you regard the audience as someone you can confide in and someone who won't judge you. (See note on talking to the audience in the introduction.)

- She is very honest and open. Without becoming overly emotional, see if you can connect to that passionate, trusting and vulnerable part of her character.

- Although her heart is broken, she can see the funny side. Look for where the speech is humorous and be aware of any irony. She understands just how typical this kind of thing is and how easily she has been duped. Notice the way she says, 'His name was Emmanuel, *of course…*' as if she should have seen it coming.

- You will need to have a very strong image in your head about what Emmanuel looks and sounds like. Perhaps you have experienced a similar 'love at first sight' attraction. How did it make you feel?

- If you can't do the Australian accent, why don't you replace the 'Hallett Cove' with the name of a small town in the area that you come from. If you are from the UK you could even change 'London' and 'Dublin' to 'Rome' and 'Venice' to make it seem more exotic/further away.

Rosie

❝ Berlin. A winter coat. A travel bag. A red nose. And a broken heart.

I'm standing on the platform at the train station. It's cold. The train is late and my socks are wet. I'm not quite sure how I got here or where I'm meant to go next.

I met him four nights ago and he was the most beautiful boy I had ever seen. His name was Emmanuel, of course, and he came from Madrid.

I'd been travelling by myself for three months. The great European adventure. London. Dublin. Paris. Prague. Then Berlin. I'd been saving for a year. Café work, bar work, babysitting. Mum and Dad said don't go by yourself. It's too dangerous. Go on a tour or at least with some girlfriends.

I'll meet people. I told them. I'll be fine. But meeting people is harder than you think. I mean I did meet people, at hostels and stuff but mainly other Australians. And it was fun for a night or two. But the boys just wanted to have sex and I guess that's alright but if I wanted sex with an Australian boy I would have stayed in Hallett Cove.

So I go to the churches and the museums and the galleries and I walk through the cobbled streets and I sit in cafés trying to look mysterious and everything is so beautiful. Everything is what I was expecting it to be. And yet somehow I want it to be more. […]

I keep wondering when it will start. Life. When will life start?

And then there he is. At a club in Mitte. Dancing. With his shirt off. And I think, wow, that guy can really dance. That guy is like… fire. And then he looks over at me. Me? And

I am gone. I pretend not to be. I try to be cool. To make it seem like I'm not interested. But I am so interested. And we dance until the sun comes up. And as we come out of the club into the light, I think this is it. This is life. I am living. […]

And when he kisses me I want to cry. Because I'd never been kissed like that. Not in Hallett Cove. And I'd never been kissed where he kissed me or touched quite like that. He seemed to know things and for once it didn't seem to matter that I didn't. Three days. Three days we stayed in bed. And after three days I knew some things too. […]

On the third night I watch him sleeping and I do that thing you shouldn't do. I think about the future. I imagine taking him home to meet Mum and Dad and my sister and brothers and and and how they will all love him, like they love me. […]

Then he wakes up and he looks at me as if he knows what I'm thinking and as if he wants to get up and run so I kiss him on his lips before he can. And he smiles. And I'm gone all over again. And we make love, so tenderly, so sweetly and after, as I drift off to sleep, lying on his chest, listening to the beat of his heart, thinking I could listen to this for the rest of my life, I think is this it, is this what falling in love is?

And when I wake up in the morning he's gone… along with four hundred euros from my wallet, my iPad, my camera, my favourite scarf and a large piece of my heart. […]

I walk through the streets of Berlin. I feel small. I feel like I'm twelve years old, I feel ridiculous. I want to cry but I won't. Well I do, a bit. But not as much as I want to. I want my dad. I want my mum. I want my brothers and my sister. I want to hear them laugh and argue and fight and tease me. But I can't think of them much because if I do my chest will explode. I feel like I'm going to literally fall to pieces. That my arms are going to drop off and then my legs and my head. And so to stop myself coming apart I make a list of all the things I know… I mean actually know for certain to be true and the really frightening thing is… It's a very short list.

I don't know much at all.

But I know that at 25 Windarie Avenue, Hallett Cove, things are the same as when I left and they always will be.

And I know that I have to go home. 🙶

The Wardrobe

Sam Holcroft

TEN THINGS YOU NEED TO KNOW ABOUT DIDO:

- Dido Elizabeth Belle was a real person.

- She was the illegitimate daughter of Sir John Lyndsay, a British Navy captain, and an enslaved woman whom Sir John encountered when his ship was in the Caribbean.

- She was dual-heritage, with a white father and a black mother.

- In the play she is thirteen, but you can play her older if you like.

- Dido lived in the house of her great-uncle William Murray, Lord Mansfield.

- The house, called Kenwood House, in Hampstead, north London, still exists today and is open to visitors.

- Also in the house is Lady Elizabeth Murray, who was the orphaned niece of Lord and Lady Mansfield.

- Dido was part companion to Elizabeth and part lady's maid.

- There is a famous painting of Dido and of Lady Elizabeth Murray where they appear to be equal. It inspired the film *Belle*, which you might like to watch.

- The scene is set in 1780. Ten years ago, Lord Mansfield, a leading judge, passed a famous judgement in court freeing a slave from imprisonment by his master on the basis that slavery was unsupported by law in England and Wales. However, it did not put an end to slavery altogether.

FIVE THINGS TO HELP YOU PERFORM THE MONOLOGUE:

- You will need to find the conflict Dido feels about being grateful that she has been rescued from slavery, but also resentful that she does not have the same rights as Elizabeth.

Perhaps you have experienced a similar kind of prejudice yourself. If not, think about that time in history when to be both illegitimate and mixed-race would have been considered shameful.

- What happens when we deny our angry feelings about things? How long does it take for those true feelings to surface and to boil over? It is hard for Dido to remain wholly grateful, and the more she tries, the more her anger bubbles up until she finally snaps.

- Find a way of being in the wardrobe. If you don't have a real piece of furniture, you could try practising the scene under a table or in some other limited space. If you are using the speech for an audition, and don't want the hassle of physically creating the wardrobe, you will have a memory of what it feels like to be cramped, which you can recreate in your acting.

- See if you can imagine the beautiful dresses that are hanging in the wardrobe. Perhaps they are rich silks and velvets. What colours come to mind? How might they feel to the touch and how might they smell? Even if you are not using a real wardrobe or clothes rail, it would be good to have some items on real hangers next to you, so that when you practise that bit in the speech, you don't have to pretend or mime pulling the dresses off the hangers. If you are using the speech for an audition, and don't want the hassle of the clothes, you will have a memory of what they feel like to the touch, as with the wardrobe itself.

- Have a picture in your head about what Uncle William and Elizabeth look like. See if you can imagine 'Fat Charlie' the pigeon. Take time to look up pictures of Kenwood House (visit if you can) so that you can really picture what the rooms look like and how you would spend your days.

Dido

66 Dear God, my heavenly father, thank you for today. Thank you for the good weather we enjoyed and for the birds outside my window. Thank you most especially for the fat pigeon that comes to rest in the old oak. I have named him Charlie. Fat Charlie. Thank you for coffee – powerful, rich coffee. I'm grateful for the strong flavour that cuts through my sluggish morning mouth. I'm grateful for the two hours' work I did this morning. I'm grateful for the pages I edited, and the progress I helped Uncle William to make with his accounts. I'm grateful that you can't get lead poisoning from stabbing yourself with a pencil. Thank you for that lovely moment just now when I mouthed to Uncle William, 'I love you,' and he mouthed in return, 'I love you too, my dear.' I am so grateful to have the love of this family. What else…? Oh yes, I'm so grateful that I am no longer scared of bees. And thank you for this beautiful wardrobe, which my uncle gave to me so I might hang my beautiful clothes in here. Thank you for the smell of the wood, and the reassuring feel of the panels under my knees holding me up. Thank you for a place I can come to when I need to be alone. Thank you also for the fact I could talk to Elizabeth for an hour about her upcoming trip to the Derby race and I didn't feel hopelessly dissatisfied that I will not attend. I am learning that the secret to happiness is not how successful you are, or what people say about you, or how you look, or whether your parents were married, but whether or not you can be thankful for what you have. And so, right now, in this moment, I am grateful to my uncle and his wife for all they have done for me and rescued me from. Today I am so grateful that I am not enslaved upon a ship, as my mother was. I am so grateful to my uncle that he struck down slavery in court. And because of him I live without fear of torture and oppression. I don't know why I've been dealt such a fortunate hand, but to whomever is responsible for my lucky, lucky fate I am truly, truly thankful. Even though my illegitimacy and the colour of my skin mean that I am not eligible to eat with the family at the table, or join their guests for dinner, or attend the Derby with Elizabeth, I am so

thankful that the women do invite me to join them for coffee when supper is done. I am so grateful they afford me that kindness; they show me such unwavering generosity.

Suddenly she pulls a dress violently off a hanger and throws it down; she smacks the wall of the wardrobe in distress. She cradles her injured hand. She catches her breath. She clasps her hands in prayer once again.

Forgive me, Father, forgive my ungratefulness. Forgive my indulgence, my impatience, my selfishness. (*Short pause.*) I'm grateful to the concept of gratefulness for giving me a way to encourage happy thoughts and feelings. Thank you for giving me a way out of the dark and into the light. **"**